Federal Funding and National Priorities

PRAEGER SPECIAL STUDIES IN
U.S. ECONOMIC AND SOCIAL DEVELOPMENT

Federal Funding
and National Priorities

AN ANALYSIS OF PROGRAMS, EXPENDITURES,
AND RESEARCH AND DEVELOPMENT

Leonard Lederman
Margaret Windus

Prepared with the assistance of
Battelle Memorial Institute, Columbus Laboratories

PRAEGER PUBLISHERS
New York • Washington • London

The purpose of Praeger Special Studies is to make specialized research in U.S. and international economics and politics available to the academic, business, and government communities. For further information, write to the Special Projects Division, Praeger Publishers, Inc., 111 Fourth Avenue, New York, N.Y. 10003.

PRAEGER PUBLISHERS
111 Fourth Avenue, New York, N.Y. 10003, U.S.A.
5, Cromwell Place, London S.W.7, England

Published in the United States of America in 1971
by Praeger Publishers, Inc.

Library of Congress Catalog Card Number: 70-136145

Printed in the United States of America

PREFACE

Although the subject of national goals and priorities has
been discussed and written about for a long period of time, it
is only within the last few years that it has become the focus
of a great deal of public attention and concern. Today, much
of the discussion and debate has turned from the more pious
pronouncements on broad goals to the more tangible and specific concern with priorities among goals and the allocation
of resources.

This concern for the nation's goals, objectives, and priorities has recently affected the scientific and technological community in a profound way. After years of acceptance and significantly increased funding of research and development
(R&D), important and serious questions have been raised about
the relationship between R&D and our national priorities. A
whole new field called science and technology policy has arisen,
and many universities and research organizations are giving
concerted attention to this subject.

At the national level, a host of new activities have started,
indicating growing attention to serious study and analysis of
national goals and priorities and the allocation of resources to
their accomplishment. These activities range from the White
House National Goals Research Staff to the pervasive and man-
datory use of the planning, programming, and budgeting system.

The scope of this book is the Government's allocation of
fiscal resources as an indicator of implicit priorities and the
relationship of R&D funding to these priorities. The purpose is
to present the trends in the allocation of Federal resources as
a foundation for a more meaningful discussion of Government
policy with regard to goals and priorities. This volume is
based upon the philosophy that analysis of trends in the allocation of Government resources and their relationship to goals
and priorities is a necessary prerequisite for examining many
of the issues surrounding public policy.

The work described in this volume represents the first
comprehensive effort to relate Federally sponsored R&D to
functional end-use purposes, goals, and objectives. It is

designed to provide a factual and objective orientation to past and current trends and to explore the likely future based on past and present priorities. It examines the Federal Government's allocation of resources and highlights what is, not necessarily what should be.

Even in speculating about the likely future, the approach used refrains from normative judgments and simply indicates what is likely to occur if past and present priorities continue. This is not to say that the nation should, or will, continue in the same way; rather, this book provides a factual basis for analyzing what has happened and what is likely to happen so that more knowledgeable public discussions can proceed on the question of future priorities and the changes they imply.

The work described in this volume started several years ago under the sponsorship of the Columbus Laboratories of the Battelle Memorial Institute, whose support and encouragement the authors gratefully acknowledge. We are equally appreciative of the more recent support provided by the National Aeronautics and Space Administration (NASA), under whose auspices the first formalization and publication of some of this book was made possible. The study sponsored by NASA was issued in February, 1969, under the title, "An Analysis of the Allocation of Federal Budget Resources as an Indicator of National Goals and Priorities."* This book substantially updates, revises, and extends the concepts, data, and information contained in that report.

We would be remiss in not acknowledging the indirect, but substantial, contributions made by the oft-criticized Bureau of the Budget, now the Office of Management and Budget. The change under a Presidential reorganization plan not only provides new functions but recognizes that The Budget of the United States is as much a planning document as it is a financial document. We hope that this volume provides added demonstration of this view.

A number of individuals contributed importantly to this work. The close cooperation, guidance, and criticism provided by Bruce W. Davis and Dr. Harold A. Hovey of Battelle and Joseph E. McGolrick of NASA were of immeasurable value.

---

*Leonard L. Lederman and Margaret L. Windus, "An Analysis of the Allocation of Federal Budget Resources as an Indicator of National Goals and Priorities," National Aeronautics and Space Administration Report No. BMI-NLVP-TR-69-1 (Columbus, Ohio: Battelle Memorial Institute, Columbus Laboratories, 1969). Available from U.S. Government Printing Office, Washington, D.C.

In addition, the encouragement and guidance provided by
Frederick L. Bagby and Dr. Duane N. Sunderman of Battelle,
Joseph B. Mahon of NASA--and, especially, Dr. William J.
Harris, Jr., formerly of Battelle and now with the Association
of American Railroads--are gratefully acknowledged. Finally,
the substantial staff support in data gathering, statistical functions, editing, and typing results from the skill, loyalty, and
service provided by Frances Rossiter, Louise Gilkerson,
Marjory Grieser, and Nancy Seale.

Needless to say, the judgments expressed and conclusions
drawn in this book are the responsibility of the authors alone
and should not be attributed to the sponsoring organizations or
persons acknowledged above.

CONTENTS

Chapter   Page

LIST OF TABLES

xvii

LIST OF FIGURES

LIST OF ABBREVIATIONS

AEC   Atomic Energy Commission

AID   Agency for International Development

CSC   Civil Service Commission

DOD   Department of Defense

DOT   Department of Transportation

FDA   Food and Drug Administration

FY   Fiscal Year

HEW   Department of Health, Education, and Welfare

LEAA   Law Enforcement Assistance Administration

NASA   National Aeronautics and Space Administration

NIH   National Institutes of Health

NSF   National Science Foundation

OASDI   Old-Age, Survivors, and Disability Insurance

OEO   Office of Economic Opportunity

PHS   Public Health Service

RRB   Railroad Retirement Board

R&D   Research and Development

RDT&E   Research, Development, Test, and Evaluation

TVA   Tennessee Valley Authority

USIA   United States Information Agency

VA   Veterans Administration

GLOSSARY

Sources: Most of the data appearing in this book were
obtained from The Budget of the United States Government
(hereafter referred to as The Budget), as were the definitions
given here. The Budget covers all Federal agencies and programs, no matter how funded. It covers both Federal funds
and trust funds. All data obtained from The Budget are from
actual fiscal years (FY's) 1961-69 and estimates for FY's
1970 and 1971. FY 1970 (ended June 30, 1970) was still subject to Administrative changes when the FY 1971 budget was
printed; FY 1971 data are requests of the President for July 1,
1970, through June 30, 1971, which are then subject to
Congressional and Administrative changes. All designations
of years with respect to data are fiscal years.

Outlays: Outlays are the liquidation of obligations made,
primarily, by the issuance of checks. Outlays consist of lending operations and expenditures.

Offsetting of receipts: All figures used are net of receipts,
such as refunds, reimbursements, and collections of revolving funds, management funds, and trust revolving funds. Receipts that arise out of the proprietary activities of the
Government--that is, interest, sale of property and products,
charges for nonregulatory services, rents, royalties, and
so forth--are not counted as budget receipts but are offset
against expenditures in total for each agency and for each
function.

Research and development (R&D): As defined by The
Budget, R&D includes activities in which the primary aim is
either to develop new knowledge or to apply existing knowledge
to new areas. Excluded from this definition are expenditures
for routine testing, experimental production, information
activities, technical assistance, and training programs.

R&D conduct: All R&D expenditures, other than those for
R&D facilities and major equipment, are included in R&D conduct. Most R&D conduct data were obtained from unpublished
Government sources. Because outlays for R&D conduct are
entirely of an expenditure nature (with no lending), the term
"expenditure" is used for R&D conduct.

Trust funds: Trust funds are established to account for receipts that are held in a fiduciary capacity by the Government for use in carrying out specific purposes and programs. All other funds are Federal funds.

Consolidation of funds: Certain payments between funds are accounted for as expenditures of one fund and as receipts of another in financial statements that relate to the individual funds. When all funds are consolidated into a single schedule, as in the budget, the duplication involved in the interfund and intragovernmental transactions must be eliminated. This is generally done by deducting the amounts involved from the outlays for the agency receiving the payment. However, in a few cases where the payment is in the nature of a transfer of receipts, the deduction is made from the agency that is making payment.

In two situations, the interfund and the intragovernmental transactions are not deducted from the figures of any agency or function but appear as special deduct lines in computing total outlays. One of these situations constitutes the Government's payments as employer into trust funds for retirement of its employees. The other consists of the interest receipts of the trust funds.

Federal Funding
and National Priorities

CHAPTER 1   CONCEPTS AND METHODOLOGY

This book is an analysis of trends in the allocation of Federal expenditures and their relationship to goals and objectives. Such an analysis is a required first step toward examining many of the issues of public policy and national priorities.

The study presented here is primarily concerned with providing a factual and objective orientation to past and present goals and objectives and the allocation of fiscal resources to their accomplishment. It covers the time period of fiscal years (FY's) 1961-71--the decade of the 60's. As such, it includes the last budget prepared by the Eisenhower Administration, all of the Kennedy and Johnson administrations, and the first budget prepared by the Nixon Administration.

The purpose is to contribute to a better understanding of goals and objectives through an examination of functional end-use purposes and to explore the relationship between Federally sponsored research and development (R&D) and Government functions. In doing so, the past and present is put under a microscope in order to understand better where we have been and where we are as a basis for considering the likely future.

CONCEPTUAL FRAMEWORK

The conceptual elements on which this study is based are as follows: first, activities are goal- or objective-oriented; second, priorities exist among goals and objectives, whether explicit or implicit; and, finally, analysis of past and present goals, objectives, and priorities contributes to an understanding of the future.

Goals are "statements of highly desirable conditions toward which society should be directed,"[1] while objectives are "the stated purposes of an organization--or an individual--capable of planning and taking action to gain intended ends. They are generally more limited and more specific than broad goals,

3

and are frequently quantitative."[2] Priorities are "preferential rating, especially one that allocates rights to goods and services usually in limited supply."[3]

Actions of the Government are expressed primarily through laws passed by the legislature, administrative actions of the Executive Branch in carrying out those laws, and decisions of the judiciary in interpreting the laws. Although some actions of the Government do not directly relate to the expenditure of money, this study is based, primarily, on the allocation of Federal budget resources as an indicator of Federal activities with respect to expressed goals. These goals are grouped into areas of end-use or "functional fields," which, themselves, contribute to more general goals or "supergoals." The goals and objectives identified are based, for the most part, on Presidential messages, budget statements, and laws passed by the Congress. Although Government actions that are not directly related to expenditure of money may influence the availability of money (such as economic policy), the effects of such actions are eventually seen in Government expenditures. Other actions of Government, such as passage of an open housing law, may involve almost no expenditure of money, but still be an expression of a national goal or objective.

Although there are many ways that a Government may act and, thereby, express its goal orientations, the allocation of Federal budget resources appears to be the best reflection of Government action with respect to national goals and priorities. This was well-expressed by Melvin Anshen when he wrote: "The unique function of a public budget is to implement the conclusions of a political philosophy through the assignment of resources to their accomplishment."[4] A similar approach has been employed by sociologists for many years in analyzing family philosophy and goals,[5] and although decried by some as too materialistic, it would still seem to be the best approach for families or for nations.

Another reason for using The Budget of the United States Government[6] as a principal indicator of priorities among goals is the obvious fact that it presents a quantified, objective, and explicit measure of the allocation of resources to national goals. Thus, budgetary elements may be expressed in quantified relationship to each other, for example, in dollars and in ratios. These relationships are then an indication of priorities. The availability of this quantifiable indicator of goals was not, however, the primary reason it was chosen. Obviously, if it were not also a valid indicator, the fact that it is quantified would offer no advantage. The logic behind its validity can be expressed rather crudely, but effectively, by the adage, "Put your money where your mouth is." Despite the many state- ments made about national goals, it is usually a willingness to devote fiscal resources to these goals that signifies their real importance.

The final element of the approach used here involves the expectation that analysis of past and present actions and goals will contribute to an understanding of the likely future. This is partially expressed in the Bernard Brodie statement: "One . . . gets a better understanding of where we are now from a review of where we have recently been."[7] It is believed that this statement may be extended to include, also, a better under- standing of the probable future.

METHODOLOGY

Using the conceptual framework outlined above, similar work by others was explored to determine the extent to which previous approaches could be adapted for use. Two well-known publications on national goals are most important: Goals for Americans: Report of the President's Commission on National Goals,[8] and Goals, Priorities, and Dollars: The Next Decade.[9] The first study was done at the request of President Eisenhower and was the stimulator of subsequent public and Governmental focus and discussion of "goals." The concept of goals used in that study was broader than the one used here and encompassed such basic and fundamental goals as democracy, freedom, and equality. Because the focus of this study was primarily on a different level of goals--those for which some expression of action and resource allocation could be gathered--the set of goals used in the Goals for Americans study was not incorpo- rated here. The study is of interest, however, as a reminder of the less tangible goals which ultimately lie behind the more tangible goals that will be discussed in this book.

Leonard Lecht's book, Goals, Priorities, and Dollars: The Next Decade, is similar to this volume in its quantified treatment of goals. It deals, however, with the entire economy, including activities outside the Federal Government (e.g., consumer expenditures, state and local Government activities), whereas this study focuses on a more detailed treatment of Federal activities as an indicator of national goals. Many of the functional fields used here are the same as those used by Lecht, although defined differently. Lecht's book serves to emphasize that an examination of national goals must address the question of priorities among goals--the challenge that this volume takes up.

In conformance with the concept discussed earlier, that is, basing goal orientation on budgetary allocations, The Budget was examined. This document organizes Federal outlays by agency and by function. The arrangement by agency (or other administrative body) is largely a reflection of the historical growth and development of the administrative apparatus of the Executive Branch. Although this arrangement is indicative of lines of responsibility and authority in carrying out Government programs--and is the basis on which Congressional appropriations are made--the functional classification is most useful when discussing goals and objectives of the Federal Government. Thus, where the broad functions served by Government programs are similar (such as International Relations), they are classified together. This approach enables one to compare Government activities more easily in terms of goals, objectives, and priorities. It has been found useful by the authors mentioned above, and it was endorsed by the President's Commission on Budget Concepts. [10]

The functional fields used here are as follows:
1. National Security
2. Income Security and Welfare
3. Health
4. Education, Knowledge, and Manpower
5. Commerce, Transportation, and Communications
6. Agriculture and Rural Development
7. General Government
8. International Relations
9. Housing and Community Development
10. Natural Resources
11. Space
12. Environment.

Although some of the titles and, more importantly, some of the line items included under The Budget functions have been changed, this is, basically, the scheme used in The Budget, with the following major exceptions:
1. Environment is a functional field in this work because of the growing national attention on environmental problems, although it is not treated as a separate function in The Budget.
2. Veterans is a functional field in The Budget but not in this work, which allocates veterans' programs to other functional fields (e.g., Housing, Education, Income Security).
3. Interest on the debt is a functional field in The Budget but

is not in this work, because it has no "use" of its own.   It is, rather, a result of past and present decisions made to fund the other functions.

Thus, this book includes twelve, rather than thirteen, functional fields.   Each field is described and defined in its own chapter, and the differences between the definition of the field used here and that presented in The Budget are explained. In assigning individual line items to the twelve functional fields, the breakout used in The Budget was followed, unless there was a compelling reason for modification.

Differences of opinion can easily arise as to placement of specific line items.   Although a concerted effort was made to set up functional fields with internal consistency, the reader can examine their makeup and visualize possible changes. The crucial question the reader should address in considering such alterations is the extent to which a change would alter the general conclusions or analysis.   Such changes may be important for some purposes, but it is unlikely that they will alter the general conclusions of this study relating to national goals and priorities.

Because of the difficulties in data consistency, no attempt has been made to go beyond The Budget detail of line items in functional field assignments.   This means that some programs (e. g. , Department of Defense (DOD) health and educational efforts) are included in the functional field most appropriate to the broader budget classification of which they are a part. Programs are not static, and, over time, a program may well evolve from one functional field to another.   The nuclear reactor program of the Atomic Energy Commission (AEC), for example, is classified in the Natural Resources field, although, at its inception, it would have gone into another field because of the lack of commercial applicability.   Such a movement may well occur in the near future in other program areas (e. g. , National Aeronautics and Space Administration (NASA) Space Applications Programs).

Goals and objectives are discussed largely in terms of the functional fields (for example, one of the stated goals of the Agriculture and Rural Development field is the achievement of parity income for farmers).   Despite the decision that goals such as "freedom" and "democracy" could not be used here because of the difficulty (if not impossibility) of defining them in an operational way, an attempt is made to relate functional field goals to more general national goals.   This has been done in a descriptive, rather than quantitative, way and is based on four "major end-purposes, " suggested by Murray Weidenbaum

in a 1965 study of Congress and the Federal budget. [11] His
description of these purposes is as follows:

> What are the major end purposes for which the
> various government programs are carried on?
>   In a world of critical international tensions,
> the initial purpose that comes to mind is the pro-
> tection of the nation against external aggressors--
> to maintain the national security. A variety of
> programs is suggested, ranging from the equip-
> ping and maintaining of our own military establish-
> ment and the bolstering of the armed forces of
> other nations regarded as potential allies, to
> various types of nonmilitary competition.
>   A second basic national purpose, one also
> going back to the Constitution, is the promotion
> of the public welfare. Here, under the public
> welfare interpretation that has prevailed, we find
> the Federal Government operating in the fields of
> health, pensions, unemployment compensation,
> relief, and many other such activities.
>   A third major purpose of government pro-
> grams has received an increasing amount of
> attention in recent years--economic development.
> This area covers the various programs to develop
> natural resources and transportation, as well as
> to support education and to attempt to quicken the
> growth rate of the national economy.
>   Finally, we have the routine day-to-day opera-
> tion of the government, such as the functioning of
> the Congress and the Federal courts, the collection
> of revenues, and the payment of interest on the
> national debt. [12]

Although, in his book, Weidenbaum attempts to relate
Government expenditures to one of these four purposes, functional fields were found to be generally multiple-purpose, and,
therefore, their expenditures were not allocated to a specific
"supergoal" (as these end-purposes are called). However, an
attempt is made to indicate the supergoals to which each functional field makes its principal contributions, as shown in
Figure 1. These relationships, which are described in the
separate functional field chapters, are meant to be indicative
rather than final or exclusive. The reader could also visualize lines connecting some of the functional fields that are

FIGURE I. SCHEMATIC RELATIONSHIP OF FUNCTIONAL FIELDS TO NATIONAL GOALS

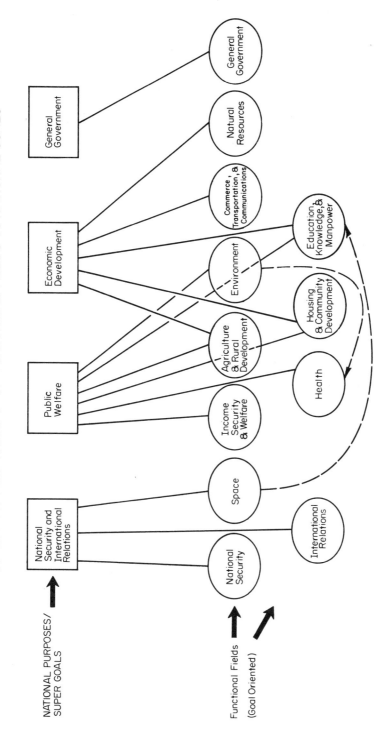

9

interrelated, such as Space with Education, Knowledge, and Manpower. A few examples of these interrelationships are shown in Figure 1.

This completes the discussion of the conceptual and methodological framework, which treats governmental activities as goal-oriented, with goals expressed descriptively in messages, laws, and so forth and quantitatively in comparative terms by the Federal budget. This budget can be broken into functional fields of activity, each field with its own goals, which, ultimately, contribute to broader national "supergoals."

PRESENTATION AND ANALYSIS

The results of the study are presented in a comparative fashion in Chapter 2, showing trends over the past decade (1961-71) and priority comparisons among the functional fields. Chapter 2 provides an overview and summary of the functional field comparisons and presents the principal findings of the study.

Chapters 3 through 14 of this book are individual chapters on each of the twelve functional fields (in descending order of total 1971 funding). Each chapter includes an introductory section on the functional field as a whole; its definition; a summary of Government interest; and trends in the allocation of Government funds to the field, to the various subfunctions and line items, and to related R&D program areas. Following this are a number of sections that describe smaller segments of the field, generally following The Budget's subfunctional structure, and a section describing the R&D program areas that relate to the field's end-purposes.

Chapter 15 concludes with a view of "The Likely Future" in terms of likely relative priorities in the next decade for the fields and the individual subfunctions.

NOTES

1. Committee for Economic Development, Research and Policy Committee, Budgeting for National Objectives (New York: Committee for Economic Development, 1966), p. 25.

2. Ibid.

3. Webster's Seventh New Collegiate Dictionary (Spring-
field, Mass.: G. & C. Merriam Co., 1963), p. 677.

4. Melvin Anshen, The Federal Budget As An Instrument
for Analysis, Planning, and Management (Santa Monica, Calif.:
The RAND Corporation, 1965), p. 21.

5. Frederic LePlay, Les Ouvriers Européens (Paris:
Alfred Mame et Fils, 1879).

6. U.S. Government, The Budget of the United States
Government, Fiscal Year 1971 (Washington, D.C.: U.S.
Government Printing Office, 1970). Referred to throughout
this book as The Budget.

7. Bernard Brodie, The American Scientific Strategists,
No. P-2979 (Santa Monica, Calif.: The RAND Corporation,
1964), p. 39.

8. The American Assembly, Goals for Americans: Report of the President's Commission on National Goals (New
York: Prentice-Hall, Inc., 1960).

9. Leonard Lecht, Goals, Priorities, and Dollars: The
Next Decade (New York: The Free Press, 1966).

10. President's Commission on Budget Concepts, Report
of the President's Commission on Budget Concepts (Washington,
D.C.: U.S. Government Printing Office, 1967).

11. Murray L. Weidenbaum, and John S. Saloma, III,
Congress and the Federal Budget (Washington, D.C.: American
Enterprise for Public Policy Research, 1965).

12. Ibid., p. 60.

CHAPTER **2** OVERVIEW AND
SUMMARY

One of the prime purposes of this study is to compare
priorities among national goals and objectives. Having explained the conceptual framework and methodology in Chapter
1, this chapter summarizes the broader comparative findings
of the study in terms of priorities. Priority indications in
this study are based on funding levels (i.e., the allocation of
Government fiscal resources) among the functional fields,
which are the mechanism for organizing national goals and
objectives.

This chapter analyzes trends over time and comparisons
among the fields for the FY 1961-71 period and the likely future.
More specific and detailed discussions of each field, including
goals, objectives, and programs make up the remaining chapters of this book.

The material in this chapter is designed to provide a summary and an overview of the past, the present, and a better
understanding of the likely future in terms of the allocations
of fiscal resources to goals and objectives and the relationship
of Government R&D efforts. All the data used are taken from
Tables 2, 3, and 4, which appear in the last section of this
chapter.

RELATIVE PRIORITIES AMONG
FUNCTIONAL FIELDS

Relative priorities among the functional fields are best
measured in terms of percent of total outlays. Such priorities
for 1971 show that for every dollar of Federal expenditures:
39¢ is spent on National Security; 30¢ on Income Security and
Welfare; 9¢ on Health; 5¢ on Education, Knowledge, and Manpower; 5¢ on Commerce, Transportation, and Communications;
and 12¢ on all other functions. The listing below shows the
twelve fields in rank order and in terms of 1971 relative priority:

12

1. National Security, 39 percent
2. Income Security and Welfare, 30 percent
3. Health, 9 percent
4. Education, Knowledge, and Manpower, 5 percent
5. Commerce, Transportation, and Communications, 5 percent
6. Agriculture and Rural Development, 3 percent
7. General Government, 2 percent
8. International Relations, 2 percent
9. Housing and Community Development, 2 percent
10. Natural Resources, 1.5 percent
11. Space, 1.5 percent
12. Environment, 0.5 percent.

Figure 2 shows trends in relative priority from 1961 through 1971 among the twelve fields. It clearly displays the significant drop in the priority of National Security. Despite the Vietnam War, National Security has become less important by 11 percent (50 percent in 1961 and 39 percent in 1971). International Relations; Commerce, Transportation, and Communications; Agriculture and Rural Development; and Natural Resources have also lost priority and are 1 percent to 2 percent less of total outlays in 1971 than in 1961.

Of the fields that have gained in priority, Health shows the largest increase, rising by 7 percent (only 2 percent in 1961 and 9 percent in 1971), largely due to Medicare and Medicaid programs. Income Security and Welfare has gained 3 percent in priority, primarily as a result of increases in Social Security payments; and Education, Knowledge, and Manpower has also increased 3 percent in priority, largely as a result of increased expenditures for elementary and secondary education, higher education, and manpower training programs. Housing and Community Development and General Government have gained in priority and are 1.5 percent and 0.6 percent more of total outlays in 1971 than 1961. Space increased by almost 4 percent up to 1966 but has lost almost 3 percent since then. The Environment field shows a small increase in percent of total (0.3 percent), but this is due to the relatively low base of this new field of growing priority. The percentage growths of air and water pollution efforts and solid waste disposal have been significant in recent years, although absolute dollars are still relatively low.

In total, there has been a significant, but not dramatic, shift in priorities from the more traditional fields of Federal activity (National Security, International Relations, Natural Resources, Agriculture, Commerce) to the fields concerned

FIGURE 2. FUNCTIONAL FIELD OUTLAYS AS PERCENT OF TOTAL OUTLAYS

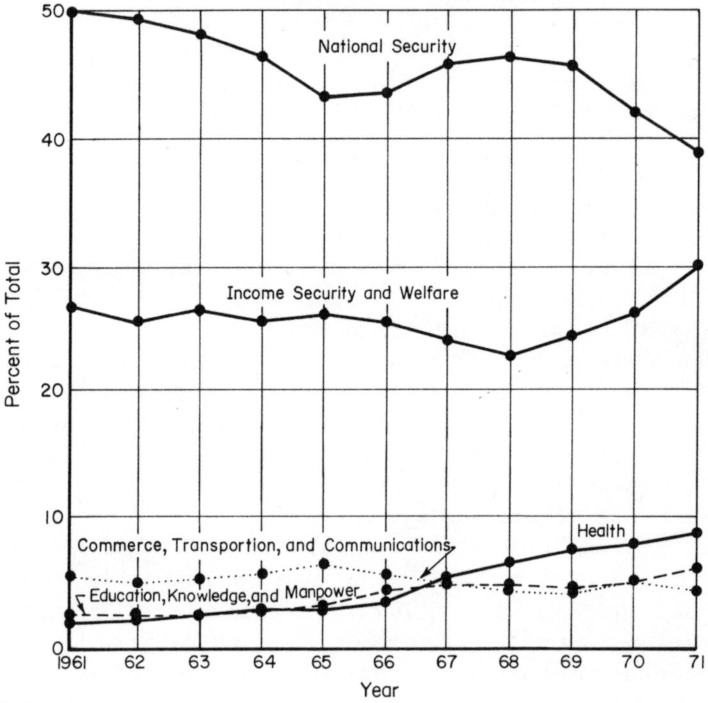

Fields with <3% in 1971 are:

	1961	62	63	64	65	66	67	68	69	70	71
Agriculture and Rural Dev.	3.6	4.1	4.9	4.6	4.3	2.9	2.9	3.5	3.6	3.4	2.9
General Government	1.6	1.6	1.7	1.8	2.0	1.8	1.7	1.5	1.6	1.9	2.2
International Relations	3.6	4.4	3.9	3.7	3.9	3.5	3.0	2.7	2.2	2.2	1.9
Housing and Community Dev.	0.4	0.8	-0.9	-0.1	0.3	2.2	2.0	2.5	1.2	1.7	1.9
Natural Resources	2.9	2.8	2.4	2.7	2.7	2.2	1.7	1.4	1.6	1.7	1.5
Space	0.5	0.9	1.9	3.1	3.9	4.1	3.1	2.4	2.1	1.7	1.5
Environment	0.2	0.2	0.2	0.2	0.3	0.3	0.3	0.3	0.3	0.3	0.5

with social problems (e. g. , Health; Income Security and Welfare; Education, Knowledge, and Manpower; Housing and Community Development).

TRENDS IN FUNCTIONAL FIELD FUNDING

Figure 3 shows the trends in absolute dollar funding for
each of the functional fields from 1961 through 1971. There
has been a major increase in outlays in the fields of Income
Security and Welfare (over $31 billion), National Security
(over $26 billion), and Health (almost $15 billion). These increases are due, primarily, to social security and public assistance payments, Vietnam War costs, and Medicare and
Medicaid health programs. In all three cases, most of the
dollar increase came in the last half of the decade, after relatively little change in the first half.

Figure 2 shows a decrease in the portion of total outlays
going to National Security, whereas Figure 3 shows a sharp
rise in funding from 1961 through 1971. This results from the
rise in funding for National Security (+57 percent) being slower
than the rise in total Federal outlays (+103 percent), and,
therefore, National Security is a lower percent of total in 1971
than in 1961. The fields of Income Security and Welfare and
Health have risen significantly, both in terms of funding and
in relative priority.

Most of the almost $8-billion growth in Education, Knowl-
edge, and Manpower came in the last half of the decade and is
a result of increased expenditures for elementary, secondary,
and higher education and manpower training. The almost $4-
billion growth in Commerce, Transportation, and Communications was fairly evenly divided between the first and last half
of the 1961-71 period and is, principally, a result of increased
outlays for air and ground transportation and area and regional
development programs. Housing and Community Development
is next in absolute growth in funding ($3 billion), primarily as
a result of increased outlays for community development and
low- and moderate-income housing programs. Outlays in the
field of General Government increased by more than $2. 5 bil-
lion, principally as a result of increased law enforcement and
central fiscal efforts. Increased outlays for farm-income
stabilization purposes largely account for the $2-billion growth
in Agriculture and Rural Development, and the development
of the Space program accounts for the over $2-billion increase

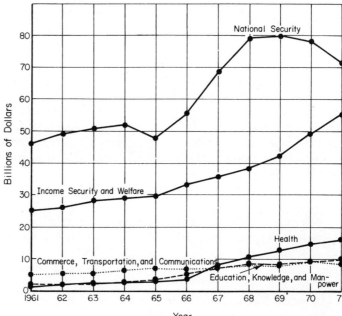

FIGURE 3. OUTLAYS BY FUNCTIONAL FIELD

Fields with <$6 billion in 1971 are :

Agriculture and Rural Dev.	3.3	4.1	5.1	5.2	4.8	3.7	4.4	5.9	6.2	6.3	5.4
General Government	1.5	1.7	1.8	2.0	2.2	2.3	2.5	2.6	2.9	3.6	4.1
International Relations	3.4	4.5	4.1	4.1	4.3	4.5	4.5	4.6	3.8	4.1	3.6
Housing and Community Dev.	0.3	0.8	-1.0	-0.1	0.3	2.8	2.9	4.3	2.1	3.2	3.5
Natural Resources	2.7	2.8	2.6	3.0	3.0	2.8	2.5	2.4	2.8	3.1	2.9
Space	0.5	0.9	2.0	3.5	4.4	5.2	4.7	4.0	3.6	3.2	2.8
Environment	0.1	0.2	0.2	0.3	0.3	0.3	0.4	0.5	0.5	0.6	0.9

16

in outlays in the Space field. Funding increases for the remaining fields are less than $1 billion each, with Environment
increasing $0.7 billion and International Relations and Natural
Resources increasing $0.2 billion each.

Only the Space and International Relations fields have experienced declines in absolute funding in the last half of the
decade. The decline in Space funding is most dramatic--de-
creasing by almost $2.5 billion since 1966--as a result of lower
manned space-flight expenditures after the initial program
buildup. International Relations funding has decreased by almost $1 billion since 1966, and Natural Resources has re-
mained relatively constant.

RELATIVE R&D PRIORITIES
AMONG FUNCTIONAL FIELDS

The listing below shows relative R&D priorities among
the twelve fields for 1971. Of every dollar of Federal R&D
expenditures: 54¢ is spent on National Security; 18¢ on Space;
8¢ on Health; 8¢ on Education, Knowledge, and Manpower; and
12¢ on R&D, principally for the end-goals and objectives of
all other functions.
 1. National Security, 54 percent
 2. Space, 18 percent
 3. Health, 8 percent
 4. Education, Knowledge, and Manpower, 8 percent
 5. Natural Resources, 5 percent
 6. Commerce, Transportation, and Communications, 3 per-
    cent
 7. Agriculture and Rural Development, 2 percent
 8. Environment, 1 percent
 9. Housing and Community Development, 0.5 percent
10. Income Security and Welfare, 0.3 percent
11. International Relations, 0.2 percent
12. General Government, 0.1 percent.

Figure 4 shows trends in relative R&D priority among the
twelve fields. It clearly displays the significant drop in the
priority of National Security R&D, especially between 1961
and 1966, and the slight increase since 1966. Over the full
time period, National Security R&D has become less important
by a significant 23 percent (77 percent in 1961 and 54 percent
in 1971). The percent of total trend line for Space is, virtually,
the mirror image of National Security--rising sharply between

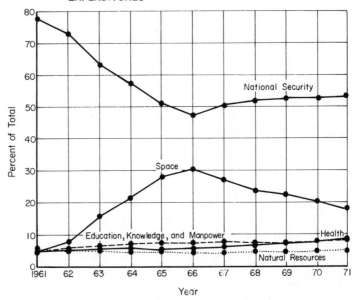

FIGURE 4. FUNCTIONAL FIELD R&D CONDUCT EXPENDITURES AS PERCENT OF TOTAL GOVERNMENT R&D CONDUCT EXPENDITURES

Fields with <3% in 1971 are:

Commerce, Transportation, and Communications	1.4	1.1	1.2	1.0	1.4	2.0	1.4	1.8	2.1	2.5	2.8
Agriculture and Rural Dev.	1.4	1.3	1.3	1.1	1.3	1.4	1.4	1.4	1.5	1.6	1.7
Environment	0.2	0.3	0.4	0.4	0.4	0.4	0.7	0.7	0.7	0.9	1.0
Housing and Community Dev.	—	*	*	*	*	0.1	0.2	0.2	0.3	0.3	0.5
Income Security and Welfare	0.1	0.1	0.1	0.1	0.2	0.3	0.3	0.3	0.3	0.3	0.3
International Relations	0.1	0.1	0.1	0.1	0.1	0.1	0.1	0.1	0.1	0.2	0.2
General Government	*	*	*	*	*	*	*	*	*	0.1	0.1

* Less than 0.05

18

1961 and 1966 and declining significantly since 1966. Space
was less than 5 percent of total R&D in 1961, building up to
31 percent in 1966 and declining to 18 percent in 1971. The
inverse relationship between National Security and Space R&D
expenditures as a percent of total is understandable, inasmuch
as together they accounted for 82 percent of total R&D in 1961
and 72 percent in 1971.

Health R&D gained 4 percent in priority; Education, Knowledge, and Manpower increased 3 percent; Commerce, Transportation, and Communications gained a little over 1 percent;
and all other fields (except Natural Resources) increased in
R&D priority, but less than 1 percent each. Natural Resources
lost 1 percent in percent of R&D expenditures between 1961
and 1971.

TRENDS IN R&D FUNDING

Figure 5 shows the trends in absolute R&D dollar funding
for each of the functional fields from 1961 through 1971. The
largest increase in R&D expenditures has been in the Space
field, which increased over $2 billion from 1961 through 1971.
However, this increase came entirely in the first half of the
decade, when Space R&D funding grew by over $4 billion during
the buildup of the Space program, especially, Manned Space
Flight. Since 1966, Space R&D expenditures have decreased
by almost $2 billion.

The second largest increase in R&D expenditures is for
National Security, which rose by $1.4 billion during 1961-1971.
The major part of this increase is a result of increased R&D
expenditures in DOD Aircraft and Related Equipment efforts
and the AEC's Special Nuclear Materials Program. Figure
4 showed a sharp decrease in the portion of total R&D expenditures going to National Security, whereas Figure 5 shows a
significant rise in absolute dollars. This results from the
rise in funding for National Security R&D (+20 percent) being
slower than the rise in total Federal R&D expenditures (+71
percent) and, therefore, National Security R&D is a lower
percent of the total in 1971 than in 1961.

The $849-million growth in Health R&D resulted primarily
from steady increases in the R&D efforts of the National Institutes of Health (NIH) and the Health Services and Mental
Health Administration through 1968, with little growth since.
This is also true of Education, Knowledge, and Manpower R&D,

which experienced all of the $775-million increase in R&D prior to 1967, largely as a result of increased funding for the Basic Research Grant program of the National Science Foundation (NSF), the Scientific Investigations in Space of NASA, the Office of Education's research efforts, and the manpower training R&D of the Office of Economic Opportunity (OEO).

The $305-million growth in Commerce, Transportation, and Communications R&D was fairly evenly divided between the first and last half of the decade and is, principally, a result of increased expenditures for aviation technology. Natural Resources R&D is next in absolute growth ($198 million), primarily due to water resources and saline water conversion efforts. R&D expenditures in the field of Agriculture and Rural Development increased by $139 million, mainly as a result of the programs of the Agricultural Research Service. Increased R&D expenditures for water and air pollution and solid waste disposal largely account for the $127-million growth in Environment R&D. R&D funding increases for the remaining fields are less than $100 million each from 1961 through 1971. While these are relatively small compared to the large R&D fields, they are significant increases in terms of the much lower base for the fields of Housing and Community Development (+$73 million), Income Security and Welfare (+$40 million), International Relations (+$23 million), and General Government (+$16 million).

COMPARISON OF TOTAL OUTLAYS AND R&D EXPENDITURES

It should be clear from the preceding that budget resource allocations by functional field for total outlays and R&D expenditures are very different. This is not surprising because we should expect the importance of R&D to the various functional fields to differ. Nonetheless, a comparison of total outlays and R&D expenditures is useful and provides some insights into the question of how the nation's scientific and technological resources can contribute more to national goals and objectives.

A useful way to compare the allocation of budget resources by functional field for total outlays and R&D expenditures is to express R&D expenditures as a percent of total outlays (i.e., the portion of total budget resources spent on R&D). The figures in Table 1 show this relationship for 1961, 1971, and the change between 1961 and 1971.

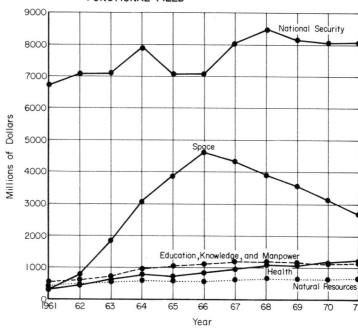

FIGURE 5. GOVERNMENT R&D CONDUCT EXPENDITURES BY FUNCTIONAL FIELD

Fields with < $500 million in 1971 are:

Commerce, Transportation, and Communications	120	103	138	141	189	301	226	295	322	382	425
Agriculture and Rural Dev.	120	132	143	157	177	211	220	233	236	241	259
Environment	18	31	40	53	55	61	114	107	116	131	145
Housing and Community Dev.	—	*	*	*	3	9	25	26	41	42	73
Income Security and Welfare	9	11	15	20	30	39	41	44	41	46	49
International Relations	5	7	13	9	11	15	18	17	15	24	28
General Government	1	2	2	2	3	*	4	2	6	9	17

* Less than $0.5 million

21

TABLE 1

R&D Conduct Expenditures as a Percent of Outlays by Functional Field, FY's 1961 and 1971

Functional Field[a]	R&D Conduct Expenditures as a Percent of Total Outlays		Change 1971 minus 1961
	1961	1971	
National Security	14.7	11.2	- 3.5
Income Security and Welfare	0.1[b]	0.1	+ 0.1
Health	20.3	7.5	-12.8
Education, Knowledge, and Manpower	18.9	12.0	- 6.9
Commerce, Transportation, and Communications	2.4	4.8	+ 2.4
Agriculture and Rural Development	3.6	4.8	+ 1.2
General Government	0.1	0.4	+ 0.3
International Relations	0.1	0.8	+ 0.7
Housing and Community Development	--	2.1	+ 2.1
Natural Resources	19.3	24.8	+ 5.5
Space	85.7	98.0	+12.3
Environment	12.8	17.0	+ 4.2
Total Government	9.5	8.0	- 1.5

[a]In 1971 outlay order.
[b]Figure is rounded.

Source: Data compiled from The Budget, FY 1961 and FY 1971.

In total, the Federal Government allocated 9.5¢ out of every dollar to R&D in 1961 but only 8¢ in 1971. This does not mean that the Government is spending less on R&D, but rather that the rate of increase in total outlays (+103 percent) has exceeded the rate of increase in R&D (+71 percent) from 1961 through 1971. While R&D expenditures have increased by over $6 billion, it is clear that, relative to all other types of Federal expenditures, R&D has suffered a significant reduction in priority over the decade.

The following fields place a higher priority on R&D than the average for the Government as a whole in 1971: Space (98¢ out of every dollar goes for R&D); Natural Resources (25¢); Environment (17¢); Education, Knowledge, and Manpower (12¢); and National Security (11¢). R&D in the Health field (7.5¢) indicates about the same priority as the Government average (8¢). All of the remaining fields place a significantly lower priority on R&D than the Government average in 1971: Commerce, Transportation, and Communications (5¢ out of every dollar goes for R&D); Agriculture and Rural Development (5¢); Housing and Community Development (2¢); International Relations (0.8¢); General Government (0.4¢); and Income Security and Welfare (0.1¢).

There has been a considerable change in the importance attached to R&D by the various fields. In every one of the six fields that placed a lower than average priority on R&D in 1961, the percent of total outlays devoted to R&D has increased from 1961 to 1971. In half of the fields that devoted a higher-than-average percent of total fiscal resources to R&D in 1961 (National Security; Health; and Education, Knowledge, and Manpower), the percent is lower in 1971. For example, 20¢ out of every dollar of Health outlays in 1961 went for R&D, while only 7.5¢ out of every dollar in 1971 was allocated to R&D. While Health R&D expenditures have increased dramatically (217 percent) between 1961 and 1971, other Health activities, such as the financing of health care (e.g., Medicare, Medicaid), have increased even more (+716 percent) and, accordingly, the percent of total Health outlays devoted to R&D has dropped.

In total, the data shows a significant reordering of relative priorities in the importance with which R&D is viewed as a contributor to the goals and objectives of the various fields. The statistical evidence for this reordering is the fact that the 1971 figures for R&D as a percent of outlays show considerably less dispersion around the mean than do the 1961 figures. The more qualitative aspects of this change are discussed in the individual functional field chapters.

TABLE 2

Budget Outlays by Function, FY's 1961-71

Functional Field	Outlays in Millions of Dollars										
	1961	1962	1963	1964	1965	1966	1967	1968	1969	1970[a]	1971[a]
National Security	46,023	49,695	50,878	52,210	48,265	55,582	68,949	79,283	80,013	78,199	72,377
Income Security and Welfare	25,045	26,350	28,235	29,162	29,845	33,129	35,776	38,558	42,671	49,564	56,173
Health	1,935	2,254	2,564	2,989	3,022	3,878	8,104	11,124	13,219	14,977	16,652
Education, Knowledge, and Manpower	2,307	2,410	2,499	2,942	3,466	5,475	7,367	8,339	8,256	9,295	10,060
Commerce, Transportation, and Communications	5,025	5,353	5,670	6,399	7,288	7,058	7,467	8,001	7,862	9,423	8,770
Agriculture and Rural Development	3,340	4,123	5,139	5,185	4,807	3,679	4,376	5,943	6,221	6,343	5,364
General Government	1,491	1,650	1,810	2,040	2,210	2,292	2,510	2,561	2,866	3,620	4,084
International Relations	3,357	4,492	4,115	4,117	4,340	4,490	4,547	4,619	3,785	4,113	3,589
Housing and Community Development	343	825	- 989	- 141	288	2,813	2,920	4,286	2,063	3,208	3,466
Natural Resources	2,667	2,814	2,562	2,993	2,985	2,804	2,523	2,398	2,776	3,091	2,882
Space	461	867	2,033	3,489	4,371	5,194	4,660	4,009	3,623	3,227	2,765
Environment	141	171	225	267	291	336	402	468	526	615	853
Total	92,135	101,004	104,741	111,652	111,178	126,730	149,601	169,589	173,881	185,675	187,035
Interest	8,108	8,321	9,215	9,810	10,357	11,285	12,588	13,744	15,791	17,821	17,799
Special Allowances[b]	---	---	---	---	---	---	---	---	---	475	2,575
Undistributed Adjustments	-2,449	-2,513	-2,644	-2,877	-3,109	-3,364	-3,936	-4,499	-5,117	-6,088	-6,639
GRAND TOTAL	97,795	106,813	111,311	118,584	118,430	134,652	158,254	178,833	184,556	197,885	200,771

Percent of Subtotal

Functional Field	1961	1962	1963	1964	1965	1966	1967	1968	1969	1970[a]	1971[a]
National Security	50.0	49.2	48.6	46.8	43.4	43.9	46.1	46.8	46.0	42.1	38.7
Income Security and Welfare	27.2	26.1	27.0	26.1	26.8	26.1	23.9	22.7	24.5	26.7	30.0
Health	2.1	2.2	2.4	2.7	2.7	3.1	5.4	6.6	7.6	8.1	8.9
Education, Knowledge, and Manpower	2.5	2.4	2.4	2.6	3.1	4.3	4.9	4.9	4.7	5.0	5.4
Commerce, Transportation, and Communications	5.5	5.3	5.4	5.7	6.6	5.6	5.0	4.7	4.5	5.1	4.7
Agriculture and Rural Development	3.6	4.1	4.9	4.6	4.3	2.9	2.9	3.5	3.6	3.4	2.9
General Government	1.6	1.6	1.7	1.8	2.0	1.8	1.7	1.5	1.6	1.9	2.2
International Relations	3.6	4.4	3.9	3.7	3.9	3.5	3.0	2.7	2.2	2.2	1.9
Housing and Community Development	0.4	0.8	-0.9	-0.1	0.3	2.2	2.0	2.5	1.2	1.7	1.9
Natural Resources	2.9	2.8	2.4	2.7	2.7	2.2	1.7	1.4	1.6	1.7	1.5
Space	0.5	0.9	1.9	3.1	3.9	4.1	3.1	2.4	2.1	1.7	1.5
Environment	0.2	0.2	0.2	0.2	0.3	0.3	0.3	0.3	0.3	0.3	0.5
Total	100.0	100.0	100.0	100.0	100.0	100.0	100.0	100.0	100.0	100.0	100.0

[a] Estimate.

[b] Special Allowances. Lump-sum allowances were included to cover possible additional supplemental proposals that might be required for 1970 and 1971. The need for such supplementals might arise from requirements not foreseen for existing programs or from the enactment of legislation not specifically provided for in the budgets of the agencies concerned.

Source: Data compiled from The Budget, FY's 1961-71.

TABLE 3

R&D Conduct Expenditures by Function, FY's 1961-71

Functional Field	Expenditures in Millions of Dollars										
	1961	1962	1963	1964	1965	1966	1967	1968	1969	1970a	1971a
National Security	6,747.4	7,138.2	7,117.5	7,867.5	7,100.2	7,158.3	8,051.7	8,486.5	8,232.0	8,062.3	8,112.8
Income Security and Welfare	8.7	11.4	15.4	19.8	30.0	39.3	41.1	43.6	40.9	46.4	49.4
Health	392.1	498.7	623.3	779.6	706.5	829.4	968.0	1,122.6	1,116.7	1,198.6	1,240.7
Education, Knowledge, and Manpower	436.2	601.1	764.7	971.0	1,032.6	1,115.2	1,228.4	1,222.8	1,154.1	1,197.0	1,210.6
Commerce, Transportation, and Communications	119.5	103.0	138.1	140.7	189.2	301.1	226.2	294.8	322.1	382.4	424.5
Agriculture and Rural Development	120.1	132.2	143.0	156.6	176.8	211.0	220.1	232.5	235.7	240.8	258.7
General Government	1.0	1.6	1.5	1.6	2.7	0.4	3.6	1.8	6.0	9.0	17.3
International Relations	4.6	7.1	12.7	9.3	10.8	14.5	18.0	16.6	14.9	24.3	27.5
Housing and Community Development	- -	0.3	0.2	0.3	2.5	8.9	24.5	26.0	41.4	41.8	73.3
Natural Resources	515.7	505.3	589.1	631.0	626.5	608.6	650.0	713.5	681.3	681.3	713.5
Space	395.0	774.6	1,833.2	3,091.6	3,858.9	4,636.4	4,383.8	3,889.6	3,570.5	3,178.4	2,708.8
Environment	18.2	31.4	40.2	52.6	54.9	60.6	114.3	107.4	115.7	131.2	145.1
Total	8,758.5	9,804.9	11,278.9	13,721.6	13,791.6	14,983.7	15,929.7	16,157.7	15,531.3	15,193.5	14,982.2

Functional Field	1961	1962	1963	1964	1965	1966	1967	1968	1969	1970[a]	1971[a]
					Percent of Total						
National Security	77.0	72.8	63.1	57.3	51.5	47.8	50.5	52.5	53.0	53.1	54.1
Income Security and Welfare	0.1	0.1	0.1	0.1	0.2	0.3	0.3	0.3	0.3	0.3	0.3
Health	4.5	5.1	5.5	5.7	5.1	5.5	6.1	6.9	7.2	7.9	8.3
Education, Knowledge, and Manpower	5.0	6.1	6.8	7.1	7.5	7.4	7.7	7.6	7.4	7.9	8.1
Commerce, Transportation, and Communications	1.4	1.1	1.2	1.0	1.4	2.0	1.4	1.8	2.1	2.5	2.8
Agriculture and Rural Development	1.4	1.3	1.3	1.1	1.3	1.4	1.4	1.4	1.5	1.6	1.7
General Government	[b]	[b]	[b]	[b]	[b]	[b]	[b]	[b]	[b]	0.1	0.1
International Relations	0.1	0.1	0.1	0.1	0.1	0.1	0.1	0.1	0.1	0.2	0.2
Housing and Community Development	- -	[b]	[b]	[b]	[b]	0.1	0.2	0.2	0.3	0.3	0.5
Natural Resources	5.9	5.2	5.2	4.6	4.5	4.1	4.1	4.4	4.4	4.5	4.8
Space	4.5	7.9	16.3	22.5	28.0	30.9	27.5	24.1	23.0	20.9	18.1
Environment	0.2	0.3	0.4	0.4	0.4	0.4	0.7	0.7	0.7	0.9	1.0
Total	100.0	100.0	100.0	100.0	100.0	100.0	100.0	100.0	100.0	100.0	100.0

[a]Estimate.
[b]Less than 0.05 percent.

Source: Data compiled from The Budget, FY's 1961-71.

TABLE 4

Comparison by Functional Field--Total Outlays and R&D Conduct Expenditures,
FY's 1961 and 1971
(In Millions of Dollars)

| Functional Field | Total Budget Outlays | | | | R&D Conduct Expenditures | | | | Percent of Total 1961 | | Percent of Total 1971 | |
| | 1961 | | 1971[a] | | 1961 | | 1971[a] | | | | | |
	Rank	Dollars	Rank	Dollars	Rank	Dollars	Rank	Dollars	Outlays	R&D	Outlays	R&D
National Security	1	46,023	1	72,377	1	6,747	1	8,113	50.0	77.0	38.7	54.1
Income Security and Welfare	2	25,045	2	56,173	9	9	10	49	27.2	0.1	30.0	0.3
Health	8	1,935	3	16,652	5	392	3	1,241	2.1	4.5	8.9	8.3
Education, Knowledge, and Manpower	7	2,307	4	10,060	3	436	4	1,211	2.5	5.0	5.4	8.1
Commerce, Transportation, and Communications	3	5,025	5	8,770	6/7	120	6	425	5.5	1.4	4.7	2.8
Agriculture and Rural Development	5	3,340	6	5,364	6/7	120	7	259	3.6	1.4	2.9	1.7
General Government	9	1,491	7	4,084	11	1	12	17	1.6	a	2.2	0.1
International Relations	4	3,357	8	3,589	10	5	11	28	3.6	0.1	1.9	0.2
Housing and Community Development	11	343	9	3,466	12	--	9	73	0.4	--	1.9	0.5
Natural Resources	6	2,667	10	2,882	2	516	5	714	2.9	5.9	1.5	4.8
Space	10	461	11	2,765	4	395	2	2,709	0.5	4.5	1.5	18.1
Environment	12	141	12	853	8	18	8	145	0.2	0.2	0.5	1.0
Total		92,135		187,035		8,759		14,982	100.0	100.0	100.0	100.0

28

Functional Field	Change in Percent of Total, 1961-71		R&D as Percent of Field		Total Outlays: 1961-71 Change		R&D Conduct: 1961-71 Change	
	Outlays	R&D	1961	1971a	Dollars	Percent	Dollars	Percent
National Security	-11.3	-22.9	14.7	11.2	+26,354	+ 57	+1,366	+ 20
Income Security and Welfare	+ 2.8	+ 0.2	b	0.1	+31,128	+124	+ 40	+444
Health	+ 6.8	+ 3.8	20.3	7.5	+14,717	+761	+ 849	+217
Education, Knowledge, and Manpower	+ 2.9	+ 3.1	18.9	12.0	+ 7,753	+336	+ 775	+178
Commerce, Transportation, and Communications	- 0.8	+ 1.4	2.4	4.8	+ 3,745	+ 75	+ 305	+254
Agriculture and Rural Development	- 0.7	+ 0.3	3.6	4.8	+ 2,024	+ 61	+ 139	+116
General Government	+ 0.6	+ 0.1	0.1	0.4	+ 2,593	+174	+ 16	+1,600
International Relations	- 1.7	+ 0.1	0.1	0.8	+ 232	+ 7	+ 23	+460
Housing and Community Development	+ 1.5	+ 0.5	- -	2.1	+ 3,123	+910	+ 73	- -
Natural Resources	- 1.4	- 1.1	19.3	24.8	+ 215	+ 8	+ 198	+ 38
Space	+ 1.0	+13.6	85.7	98.0	+ 2,304	+500	+2,314	+586
Environment	+ 0.3	+ 0.8	12.8	17.0	+ 712	+505	+ 127	+706
Total	0.0	0.0	9.5	8.0	+94,900	+103	+6,223	+ 71

a Estimate.
b Less than 0.05 percent.

Source: Data compiled from The Budget, FY 1961 and 1971.

29

BASIC DATA

The basic data on which this study is based are shown in Tables 2, 3, and 4. Table 2 gives total outlays by functional field for FY's 1961 through 1971 and percent of total for each year. Table 3 provides R&D conduct expenditures by functional field for these same years and percent of total for each year. Table 4 provides a variety of data summarizing the position of the fields in 1961 and in 1971, based on the data in Tables 2 and 3.

CHAPTER **3** NATIONAL SECURITY

THE FIELD AS A WHOLE

The functional field of "National Security" or "National Defense" in The Budget includes programs "designed to pre-serve the freedom and territorial integrity of this Nation and its allies."[1] The field encompasses all programs of DOD (except the Army Corps of Engineers, which is under Natural Resources), including military assistance, atomic energy programs, and other "defense related activities" (e. g. , stock-piling of strategic and critical materials, expansion of defense production, selective service systems, and emergency prepared-ness activities). This categorization has been modified to exclude the nonmilitary activities of the AEC, which is estimated by AEC to be about one-half of AEC's expenditures.[2] The field has been titled "National Security" here, although it is frequently referred to as "National Defense, " or, simply, "Defense. "

Responsibility for protecting and enhancing the national security of the United States was one of the earliest functions ascribed to the Federal Government and was incorporated in the Articles of Confederation and, later, the Constitution. This field is so uniquely a Federal responsibility, and so generally accepted as such, that there is no need to dwell upon its histor-ical development here or its contribution to the supergoal of National Security and International Relations. Despite general consensus on the Federal Government's unique role in National Security, there have been wide swings in interpretation of how this role should be played, running the gamut from isolation to active international involvement. However, beginning with U. S. entry into World War II and continuing through the cold war, Korean conflict, and the Vietnam War, the question of complete isolationism has died, with the focus of attention on how and to what extent to pursue national security interests and involvement.

As would be expected, because of the unique and long

historic role of the Government in this field, frequent refer-
ences are made to U. S. policies, goals, objectives, and
programs in this area in Presidential messages and in the
Congress. During the past decade, many special Presidential
messages were delivered to Congress on National Security,
plus numerous other requests, appropriations, and policy pronouncements. All Presidents during this period have, on
several occasions, sent special messages to the Congress
dealing with this field. There is little need to stress further
the focus of attention that all recent administrations, regardless of party, have placed on National Security. The most
complete and definitive unclassified document covering this
field has, in the past, been the annual "posture" statement of
the Secretary of Defense. In 1970, President Nixon issued a
first annual report on foreign policy, entitled United States
Foreign Policy for the 1970's: A New Strategy for Peace. [3]
     At the outset of his statement, President Nixon set forth
three basic principles for peace:

> I have often reflected on the meaning of 'peace.' and
> have reached one certain conclusion: Peace must be
> far more than the absence of war. Peace must pro-
> vide a durable structure of international relationships
> which inhibits or removes the causes of war. Build-
> ing a lasting peace requires a foreign policy guided
> by three basic principles:
>
> > Peace requires partnership. Its obligations,
> > like its benefits, must be shared. This con-
> > cept of partnership guides our relations with
> > all friendly nations.
> >
> > Peace requires strength. So long as there
> > are those who would threaten our vital interests
> > and those of our allies with military force, we
> > must be strong. American weakness could
> > tempt would-be agressors to make dangerous
> > miscalculations.
> >
> > At the same time, our own strength is
> > important only in relation to the strength of
> > others. We--like others--must place high
> > priority on enhancing our security through
> > cooperative arms control.
> >
> > Peace requires a willingness to negoti-
> > ate. All nations--and we are no exception--
> > have important national interests to protect.
> > But the most fundamental interest of all nations
> > lies in building the structure of peace. In

> partnership with our allies, secure in our
> own strength, we will seek those areas in
> which we can agree among ourselves and with
> others to accommodate conflicts and over-
> come rivalries. We are working toward the
> day when all nations will have a stake in
> peace, and will therefore be partners in its
> maintenance. [4]

He explained the central thesis of the "Nixon Doctrine" as being that the United States would "participate in the defense and development of allies and friends, but that America cannot-- and will not--conceive all the plans, design all the programs, execute all the decisions and undertake all the defense of the free nations of the world. "[5]

In terms of allocation of fiscal resources, National Security is clearly in first place; however, it is now less than 39 percent of all Federal outlays, compared with 50 percent in 1961, despite the cost of the Vietnam War. Table 2 shows outlays for the National Security field from 1961 to 1971 and the percent of total for each year. The highest percent was 50 percent in 1961, with a steady decrease to 43 percent in 1965. There was a rise (due to Vietnam activities) to 47 percent in 1968 and a fall to an estimated 39 percent in 1971. This decrease of 11 percent of total Government outlays allocated to National Security from 1961 to 1971 occurred, despite a growth in actual expenditures from $46 billion in 1961 to $80 billion in 1969 and then back down to an estimated $72 billion in 1971, because of the faster relative growth of other fields.

Although National Security has traditionally had a "first lien on the Treasury," the latter part of the past decade saw increased questioning of the extent of resources devoted to this function. A new willingness emerged to discuss National Security in the context of all priorities, rather than as a thing apart. DOD, whose budget requests had for many years been relatively untouchable, found itself strongly questioned by members of both parties in Congress and by the Bureau of the Budget and under pressure to reduce its own requests. The Democratic Majority Leader in the Senate said it would no longer be simply a matter of: "Ask and you shall receive. "[6] The Republican Minority Leader called for significant cuts in the defense budget to free funds for environmental problems, indicating that the Government had lost $8 billion of aircraft in Vietnam since 1964--double the amount spent on preserving a livable environment. [7] The significance of such challenges lies in the large proportion of the budget that had traditionally gone to National Security. When expenditures for National Security are no longer unchallengeable and become a part of broader discussions on national priorities, the possibilities for reallocation become significant, as the data in Chapter 2 clearly show.

The National Security field also ranks first in terms of R&D expenditures for the 1961-71 period, but its relative position is also declining. In 1961, National Security R&D expenditures were 77 percent of total Government R&D expenditures, compared with a 1971 estimate of 54 percent--a decline of 23 percent. In dollars, National Security R&D has increased from $6.7 billion in 1961 to $8.1 billion in 1971, but the overall increase in Government R&D has been much greater because of growth in other fields. Overall Government R&D funding has increased 71 percent between 1961 and 1971, while National Security R&D funding has increased 20 percent, and, as a result, National Security R&D is a lower percent of total R&D.

In importance of R&D to its respective functional field, National Security is slightly higher than the Government average, but R&D is of less importance to the field in 1971 than in 1961. On the average, the Government allocated 9.5 percent of all outlays to R&D expenditures in 1961 and 8 percent in 1971, but the National Security functional field allocated 14.7 percent of total outlays to R&D in 1961 and 11.2 percent in 1971.

Table 5 presents a more detailed look at overall expenditures for major National Security areas and shows actual 1969, and estimated 1970 and 1971, expenditures as given in The Budget.

DEPARTMENT OF DEFENSE

As the figures in Table 5 show, overall Department of Defense (DOD) expenditures for military functions are estimated at $71.1 billion for FY 1971--$6 billion less than estimated for 1970, which is less than in 1969.

For planning and allocation purposes, the resources of DOD are summarized and reviewed in terms of "major mission-oriented programs" in The Budget and the annual statement of the Secretary of Defense. This pattern for disaggregating DOD efforts will be followed here as most meaningful, although

TABLE 5

National Security Outlay Details, FY's
1969, 1970, and 1971
(In Millions of Dollars)

Program or Agency	Outlays		
	1969[a]	1970[b]	1971[b]
Department of Defense--Military:			
Military Personnel	21,374	22,301	20,911
Retired Military Personnel	2,444	2,857	3,193
Operation and Maintenance	22,227	21,500	19,650
Procurement	23,988	21,550	18,799
Research, Development, Test, and Evaluation	7,457	7,300	7,382
Military Construction	1,389	1,124	1,154
Family Housing	572	630	623
Civil Defense	87	75	70
Revolving and Management Funds and Other	-1,534	-698	-434
Military Trust Funds	10	8	8
Deductions for Offsetting Receipts	-135	-140	-163
Subtotal, Military[c]	77,877	76,505	71,191
Military Assistance:			
Grants and Credit Sales[c]	685	545	625
Trust Fund[c]	103	-50	-25
Subtotal, Military and Military Assistance[c]	78,666	77,000	71,791
Atomic Energy[c,d]	1,225	1,230	1,205
Defense-Related Activities:			
Stockpiling of Strategic and Critical Materials	18	19	23
Expansion of Defense Production	166	18	-157
Selective Service System	65	74	75
Emergency Preparedness Activities	11	8	8
Deductions for Offsetting Receipts:			
Proprietary Receipts from the Public[e]	-138	-150	-572
Total	80,013	78,199	72,377

[a]Actual.
[b]Estimate.
[c]Entries net of offsetting receipts.
[d]Includes both Federal funds and trust funds.
[e]Excludes offsetting receipts that have been deducted by subfunction above: 1969,
$1,094 million; 1970, $1,171 million; 1971, $1,179 million.
Note: Figures may not add to totals because of rounding.

Source: Edited excerpts from The Budget, FY 1971, p. 82.

it differs somewhat in arrangement from the information in
Table 5.   The funding for these major mission-oriented
program areas are summarized in Table 6 in terms of total
obligational authority (which includes the new obligational
authority enacted by the Congress each year, plus the obligational authority granted in earlier years and still available).
Following Table 6 is a brief description of each of the major
mission-oriented program areas and planned efforts.

While the broad goals and objectives in National Security
have been fairly stable over the last ten years or so, program
areas, as would be expected, have varied widely and frequently.
The subsections that summarize the elements which make up
the National Security field concentrate on the most recent
period.   This functional field is so responsive to what potential
adversaries do, or are capable of doing, that longer historical
reviews of program areas have limited utility.

Southeast Asia

Because of the critical importance of the Vietnam War to
the recent allocation of resources to the National Security
field, it is useful to look at Southeast Asia data separately.
Table 7 shows the budget expenditures attributable to Southeast Asia activities for 1969 and 1970.   (These figures are not
available for 1971.) The Southeast Asia figures shown below
are included in the various line items shown on the previous
two tables.   Even when the nondirect Vietnam War costs (base-
line force) are excluded, the figures indicate that the cost of
Southeast Asia operations was 23 percent of DOD military
costs in 1970.

Strategic Forces

Strategic forces are designed to constitute a deterrent to
nuclear aggression against the United States and its allies.
To accomplish this goal, the objective has been the creation
and maintenance of varied, reliable, and credible strategic
forces, capable of withstanding surprise attacks and retali-
ating with such power that a potential enemy would not engage
in a first-strike.   As expressed by the Nixon Administration,
this means a strategic goal of "sufficiency," which means that
"we must insure that all potential aggressors see unacceptable
risks in contemplating a nuclear attack, or nuclear blackmail,

TABLE 6

Summary of the Department of Defense
Budget Program, FY's 1969, 1970, and 1971
(In Billions of Dollars)

Major Military Programs	Total Obligational Authority		
	1969[a]	1970[b]	1971[b]
Strategic Forces	8.6	7.5	7.9
General Purpose Forces	30.7	27.8	24.7
Intelligence and Communications	5.8	5.6	5.2
Airlift and Sealift	1.6	1.7	1.5
Guard and Reserve Forces	2.1	2.5	2.5
R&D	4.7	4.8	5.4
Central Supply and Maintenance	9.4	9.4	8.4
Training, Medical, and Other General Personnel Activities	12.4	13.0	12.6
Administration and Associated Activities	1.3	1.5	1.5
Support of Other Nations	2.2	2.4	2.5
Total Obligational Authority	78.7	76.4	72.3
Of Which:			
New Budget Authority	77.0	73.5	70.8
Prior Year Funds and Other Financial Adjustments	-1.7	-2.9	-1.5

[a] Actual.
[b] Estimate.
Note: Figures may not add to totals because of rounding.

Source: The Budget, FY 1971, p. 84

TABLE 7

Southeast Asia and Other Costs, FY's 1969-71

(In Millions of Dollars)

Costs	Outlays		
	1969	1970	1971
Southeast Asia (Full Costs)	28,805	23,204	---
Less Costs Also Applicable to Baseline Force	-7,261	-5,776	---
Southeast Asia (Incremental Costs)	21,544	17,428	---
Baseline Force Costs	57,122	59,572	---
Total	78,666	77,000	71,791

Source: U.S. Congress, House Committee on Appropriations, Subcommittee on Department of Defense, "Hearings on Department of Defense Appropriations for 1971," Pt. 1, 91st Congress, 2nd Sess. (Washington, D.C.: U.S. Government Printing Office, 1970), p. 488.

or acts which could escalate to strategic nuclear war, such as a Soviet conventional attack on Europe. "[8]

Programs in pursuit of this goal include procuring more sophisticated land- and sea-based missiles, capable of utilizing multiple independent reentry vehicles (MIRV's); deployment of an antiballistic missile (ABM) defense system for force protection or protection from an attack from a country other than the U.S.S.R.; development of an over-the-horizon radar and airborne warning and control system; strategic bombers; and R&D.

The President's FY 1971 budget requested total obligational authority of $7.9 billion for this program area, as compared with $7.5 billion in 1970 and $8.6 billion in 1969.

General Purpose Forces

General purpose forces are tactical forces designed to deter nonnuclear military threats. Most of the forces in being are devoted to this mission. These forces are kept in readiness to be used in support of nations with whom the United States has mutual defense treaties or nations whose defense is regarded as in our vital security interests. Treaties exist with over forty other countries, although they do not necessarily specify how the United States will react to a given situation.

A change has occurred in the conceptual framework in which the general purpose forces are viewed. The "two and one-half war principle" was included in various defense posture statements in the 1960's. This concept envisioned the possibility of two major contingencies occurring simultaneously, one in Europe and one in Asia, as well as a minor contingency in a place such as Latin America. The concept has changed toward a "one and one-half war" strategy, expressed in President Nixon's foreign policy statement as: "Under it we will maintain in peacetime general purpose forces adequate for simultaneously meeting a major Communist attack in either Europe or Asia, assisting allies against non-Chinese threats in Asia, and contending with a contingency elsewhere. "[9] This strategy was based on U.S. nuclear capability to deter full-scale attacks, the reduced chances of Sino-Soviet cooperation, a desire to maintain more troops than would be necessary for just one theater, and the wish to maintain strength in general purpose forces as a deterrent.

The total obligational authority shown in Table 6 for

general purpose forces accounts for a significant part of the
total reduction in DOD estimated expenditures. It has gone
down over the 1969 through 1971 period from $31 to $25 billion
and is a reduced percent of total DOD expenditures. Total
military force strength is expected to decrease from 3,459,000
in FY 1969 to 3,161,000 in 1970 and 2,908,000 in 1971.

Intelligence and Communications

Intelligence and Communications include communications,
general space support systems, intelligence, security, weather
service, and oceanography. Total obligational authority is
estimated in The Budget at $5.2 billion for FY 1971, compared
with $5.6 billion in 1970--a 7 percent decrease.

Airlift and Sealift

Airlift and Sealift, which include transport and troop
carrier aircraft, troop and cargo ships, and stocks of equipment prepositioned overseas, are designed to move large
forces rapidly and supply them in sustained combat at great
distances. Total obligational authority is estimated at $1.5
billion for FY 1971, compared with $1.7 billion for 1970.

Guard and Reserve Forces

Guard and Reserve Forces are designed to provide trained
and equipped units capable of rapidly reinforcing regular
forces in an emergency. Total obligational authority is estimated at $2.5 billion for FY 1971, the same as in 1970.

New Systems Research and Development

R&D supports research activities and finances the development costs of new systems yet to be approved for operational
use. As used by the DOD, this major mission-oriented categorization excludes R&D for systems already approved for
procurement and places such activities in the mission-oriented
program (e.g., R&D in connection with the Safeguard system
is funded under the Strategic Forces program). (However,

because of the special interest in R&D associated with this
study, all National Security R&D programs, including those
on approved systems, are reviewed in greater detail in a later
section. The reader is referred to this section for more detailed information and data on R&D programs with the caution
that the figures are not comparable to the figures shown in
this section.) Total obligational authority for R&D associated
with systems not approved for procurement is estimated at
$5.4 billion for FY 1971, which is an increase of $0.6 billion
over 1970.

Central Supply and Maintenance

Central Supply and Maintenance involves the management
of the supply and maintenance of military equipment. Total
obligational authority for this program is estimated at $8.4
billion in FY 1971, compared with $9.4 billion in 1970.

Training, Medical, and Other
General Personnel Activities

These include the operation of general hospitals, basic
and specialized training, travel and transportation for permanent change of station, debt-service payments on family housing,
and homeowners assistance. Total obligational authority for
these activities is estimated to be $12.6 billion in FY 1971,
compared with $13 billion in 1970.

Support of Other Nations
(Military Assistance Program)

This program primarily finances grants and credit sales
for military equipment for other countries when it is considered
to be in the interest of the United States to do so. Total obligational authority is estimated at $2.5 billion for FY 1971,
compared with $2.4 billion in 1970.

ATOMIC ENERGY COMMISSION

The two AEC program areas relevant to National Security

are nuclear materials (also relevant to nonmilitary interests) and military applications. As stated earlier, AEC estimates its military activities account for one-half of total expenditures. On this basis, such activities would account for approximately $1.2 billion of total estimated expenditures in FY 1971.

The plutonium production reactors, which supply plutonium for military purposes, are being used less for this aspect than in previous years. Some have been shut down, and remaining plants serve civilian as well as military needs. The military applications programs of the AEC primarily include AEC's nuclear weapons and naval reactor programs.

RESEARCH AND DEVELOPMENT

As mentioned in the R&D section under the major mission-oriented programs discussed earlier, R&D for systems already approved for procurement were included under the category of the system rather than R&D. Because of the special interest in R&D associated with this study, this section goes into greater detail on all National Security R&D activities (including those for systems approved for procurement). The figures shown in Table 8 are those commonly referred to as Research, Development, Test, and Evaluation (RDT&E), and data are provided separately for all DOD National Security R&D program areas as well as National Security R&D outside of DOD.

Department of Defense[*]

The purposes of RDT&E are to provide scientific and technological capabilities for the development, test, and improvement of advanced weapon systems and related equipment and techniques. Many investigative and engineering activities are performed, including scientific research directly related to defense functions and operations, design and fabrication of weapons and equipment for the future, and testing of these items to evaluate their military utility.

Missiles and Related Equipment

This activity provides for RDT&E of missile systems of

---

[*]Descriptions of these R&D program areas are excerpted from The Budget.

TABLE 8

National Security R&D Conduct Expenditures
by Program Area, FY's 1969-71
(In Millions of Dollars)

Rank	Program Area	Agency	1969[a]	1970[b]	1971[b]
1	Missiles and Related Equipment	DOD	2,410.0	2,159.0	2,299.0
2	Aircraft and Related Equipment	DOD	1,031.0	1,530.0	1,489.0
3	Other Equipment	DOD	1,037.8	1,145.4	1,082.4
4	Military Astronautics and Related Equipment	DOD	1,159.0	739.0	663.0
5	Military Science	DOD	583.0	523.0	556.0
6	Special Nuclear Materials	AEC	578.0	532.0	506.0
7	Programwide Management and Support	DOD	362.4	370.0	403.1
8	Other Defense R&D	DOD	382.8	395.9	382.5
9	Ships, Small Craft and Related Equipment	DOD	329.0	290.0	368.0
10	Ordnance, Combat Vehicles	DOD	337.0	338.0	309.0
11	Emergency Fund	DOD	---	20.0	38.0
12	Other AEC R&D	AEC	12.5	13.0	10.5
13	Civil Defense		9.0	6.0	5.3
14	Office of Emergency Preparedness		0.5	1.0	1.0
	Total		8,232.0	8,062.3	8,112.8

[a] Actual.
[b] Estimate.

Source: Compiled from Department of Defense Table FAD-648 and data supplied by the Office of Management and Budget.

all types, such as the Poseidon and Minuteman. It also includes RDT&E on an undersea long-range missile system, Safeguard antiballistic missile system, advanced strike weapons, the Condor and Maverick, an antiship missile, and tactical air defense missile systems.

Aircraft and Related Equipment

This activity funds the RDT&E related to air frames, engines, and other installed aircraft equipment. Applied research in a wide variety of supporting technologies, including flight dynamics, advanced aircraft propulsion systems, avionics, and biotechnology are funded here.

Weapon systems include the Air Force B-1 advanced strategic bomber, the subsonic cruise armed decoy (SCAD), the Navy heavy lift helicopter, Navy F-14A fleet air defense fighter/interceptor and its F14B/C growth versions, the S-3A antisubmarine warfare carrier based aircraft, the Air Force F-15 air superiority fighter, the Air Force FB-111 strategic bomber, the C-5 logistic transport, and the Navy EA-6B electronic warfare aircraft.

Studies and preliminary development continue on an advanced aerial tanker, light intratheater transport, an improved air defense interceptor for the Air Force, and a Navy destroyer-based helicopter system for fleet defense.

Military Astronautics and Related Equipment

This activity provides for programs directed toward the improvement of space technology for military purposes, as well as investigations and development of specific military applications of space vehicles. Major programs include military communications satellite systems and ballistic missile early warning systems. Support is provided for flight experiment programs and ground-based applied research and technology development programs in such areas as secondary power sources and navigation, guidance, sensor, reentry, and propulsion systems. Prior to its cancellation, the Manned Orbiting Lab (MOL) was funded by this activity.

Other Equipment

This activity provides for RDT&E of equipment not separately provided for under other activities. Examples of the types of programs funded here are ocean engineering systems and technology development, chemical and biological agent detection and protective devices, combat clothing, tactical data processing systems, communications and electronic warfare equipment, improved logistics and materiel handling, mapping and geodetic systems, and biomedical projects.

Military Sciences

This activity supports research in the physical, mathematical, environmental, engineering, biomedical, and behavioral sciences, adding needed scientific knowledge leading to applications of military significance. The research tasks selected are derived from an analysis of basic missions and corresponding technological requirements, as well as from a review of technical opportunities related to national security needs.

Ordnance, Combat Vehicles, and Related Equipment

This activity provides for the development and test evaluation of improved artillery, guns, rocket launchers, mortars, small arms, mines, grenades, torpedoes, nuclear and chemical munitions, and conventional air-launched weapons, as well as exploration and evaluation of new fuzes, propellants, explosives, detonators, dispensers, armor, and propulsion.

Ships, Small Craft, and Related Equipment

This activity provides for design of new types of ships and for development of mine warfare weapons, shipboard equipment (including command and control systems), and nuclear and nonnuclear propulsion plants. Development of ship and submarine sensors and countermeasures systems and advanced surface craft development are included under this activity.

Civil Defense

This activity provides for improvement of the technical basis for ongoing and potential future civil defense programs and operations.

Programwide Management and Support

For the Army and the Navy, this activity provides for those

costs of operation, management, and maintenance of research, development, and test facilities that are not distributed directly to other budget activities. For the Air Force, it provides for certain costs of central administration, such as the Air Force systems command headquarters and divisions, as well as several large RDT&E centers.

Other

This category includes pay of military personnel performing R&D.

Emergency Fund

The Emergency Fund enables the Secretary of Defense to support the exploitation of new scientific developments and technological breakthroughs and to provide for other unforeseen contingencies in the RDT&E programs. Programs funded under this activity are later transferred to the use activity.

Other Agencies

Special Nuclear Materials and Weapons (AEC)

This activity funds work on process improvements to assure efficiency and safety of operation and to develop more economical methods of production. The weapons program encompasses the production of atomic weapons; the maintenance of stockpiled weapons in a state of constant readiness; the design, development, and underground testing of new weapons types, including the use of supplemental test sites; the conduct of an atmospheric test readiness program; and participation with DOD in the development of test detection methods.

Office of Emergency Preparedness

The Office of Emergency Preparedness (OEP) advises and assists the President with respect to nonmilitary emergency preparedness activities. This includes coordinating emergency preparedness programs of Federal departments and agencies and providing staff support and policy guidance for emergency resource management planning functions.

NOTES

1.   Executive Office of the President, Bureau of the Budget, The Budget in Brief, FY 1969 (Washington, D.C.: U.S. Government Printing Office, 1968), p. 24.

2.   Glenn T. Seaborg, The Proliferation of the Peaceful Atom, paper delivered at the 24th Annual National Conference, American Public Power Association, Denver, Colo., May 11, 1967.

3.   Richard M. Nixon, United States Foreign Policy for the 1970's: A New Strategy for Peace (Washington, D.C.: Office of the White House Press Secretary, February 18, 1970).

4.   Ibid., p. 3.

5.   Ibid., p. 5.

6.   Statement, Senator Mike Mansfield, Science (April, 1969), p. 279.

7.   Statement, Senator Hugh Scott, The Washington Post (October 28, 1969).

8.   United States Foreign Policy for the 1970's, op. cit., p. 92.

9.   Ibid., p. 98.

CHAPTER **4** INCOME SECURITY AND
WELFARE

THE FIELD AS A WHOLE

The functional field of Income Security and Welfare includes programs that provide income for the individual in
certain common situations in which he cannot provide for himself through working. [1] This category also includes similar
expenditures for communities, as in the case of disaster
relief. To the subfunctions appearing under this field in The
Budget, we have added a subfunction for veterans' income
security programs.

The distinction should be noted between the functional
field of "Income Security and Welfare" and the supergoal discussed in Chapter 1 of "Public Welfare." The functional field
of Income Security and Welfare is fairly narrowly circum-
scribed by the definition given in the first sentence above. The
supergoal "Public Welfare" is much more broadly defined, and
it is contributed to by all programs that are directed to helping
the individual as an individual, whether it be through Education,
Health, Income Security, or any other programs and functions.

The interest and involvement of the Government in this
functional field really took hold only with the Great Depression
of the 1930's, when it became clear that economic circum-
stances in an industrialized economy might result in lack of
jobs and income, despite a person's willingness and ability to
work. Before the Depression, individual economic well-being
was regarded as a personal, or family, responsibility; and,
if that failed, then it was usually considered a function of
charitable or religious organizations. It was generally accepted that persons or families could provide for themselves.
This concept had more validity when the United States was
primarily an agricultural nation with enough land for everyone
to grow food and when families generally stayed together
through many generations; older people were cared for within
the extended family grouping. The Great Depression served

to highlight the economic and social changes that were taking place, as more people depended on factory jobs and as greater mobility resulted in dispersion of families. The first far-reaching result of Governmental attempts to provide some personal economic security was the Social Security Act of 1935. The first line item in Table 9 shows the dollar commitment resulting from this program--over $33-billion estimated 1971 outlays.

In total, the 1971 estimated Income Security and Welfare outlays are $56 billion--second only to National Security in functional field outlays--accounting for 30 percent of all outlays. This is an increase of 3 percent from the 1961 percent of total figure of 27 percent, when it was also second only to National Security. In R&D conduct expenditures--all by the Health, Education, and Welfare (HEW) Social and Rehabilitation Service--Welfare has risen from $9 million in 1961 to $49 million in 1971, and it was ranked nine or ten (out of twelve) in R&D in those years. Welfare R&D was well under 1 percent of all R&D outlays in both years and, also, well under 1 percent of all Welfare outlays in both years.

Table 9 shows the actual 1969, and estimated 1970 and 1971, outlays as given in The Budget. HEW is the agency of primary responsibility and administers about $40 billion of the $56-billion total. The Civil Service Commission (CSC) and Railroad Retirement Board (RRB) manage retirement funds for Federal civil servants and railroad employees, respectively. The Labor Department manages unemployment insurance and the Veterans Administration (VA) most of the veterans' programs. The Agriculture Department handles most of the nutrition programs, such as the food stamp program.

RETIREMENT AND SOCIAL INSURANCE

Most expenditures in this subfunction are made by trust funds, that is, funds that are held in a fiduciary capacity by the the Government to be used for specified purposes. Funds are generally obtained by taxes or contributions paid by workers and employers. As has been noted, the largest item in this subfunction is Old-Age, Survivors, and Disability Insurance (OASDI), which is designed to provide individuals or families with replacement of some of the income lost because of old age, disability, retirement, or death. Coverage under this Social Security Act program has been extended to most

TABLE 9

Income Security and Welfare Outlay Details,
FY's 1969, 1970, and 1971
(In Millions of Dollars)

Program or Agency	Outlays		
	1969a	1970b	1971b
Retirement and Social Insurance:			
Old-age, Survivors, and Disability Insurance (Trust Funds): [c]			
Present programs (HEW)	26,791	29,828	33,612
Unemployment Insurance (Labor)[d]	2,286	2,898	3,246
Civil Service Retirement and Disability (Trust Fund) (CSC)[c]	1,812	2,810	3,206
Railroad Retirement (trust fund) (RRB):[c]			
Present Programs	1,498	1,636	1,712
Proposed Legislation	---	44	104
Special Benefits for Disabled Coal Miners	---	20	150
Other[d]	-147	-130	-134
Public Assistance:			
Grants to States for Public Assistance (Maintenance Assistance) (HEW)	3,618	4,339	4,847
Family Assistance, Proposed Legislation (HEW)	---	---	500
Food and Nutrition (Agriculture)	587	958	1,580
Other (HEW)	68	84	108
Social and Individual Services (mainly HEW):			
Grants to States for Public Assistance (Social Services)[e]	343	497	531
Rehabilitation Services and Facilities	353	499	562
Aging	16	28	27
Juvenile Delinquency	1	9	13
Research, Demonstration, and Training	99	93	117
Other	74	220	204
Veterans Income Security (VA):			
Compensation and Pensions:			
Service-connected compensation	2,658	2,937	3,066
Nonservice-connected pensions	2,149	2,250	2,272
Other veterans benefits and services	72	78	82
Proposed legislation[f]	---	---	-106
Insurance programs:			
National service life insurance trust fund	627	657	676
U.S. Government life insurance trust fund	76	80	78
All other insurance programs	-54	-53	-51
Other Veterans Benefits and Services:			
VA Administrative Expenses	205	236	239
Other VA Programs	1	1	*
Non-VA Veterans Support Programs	31	29	31
Deductions for Offsetting Receipts (Veterans):	-494	-485	-499
Total	42,671	49,564	56,173

[a] Actual.
[b] Estimate.
[c] Entries net of interfund and intragovernmental transactions: 1969, $955 million; 1970, $1,020 million; 1971, $1,065 million.
[d] Includes both Federal funds and trust funds.
[e] Does not include $56 million in 1969 for child welfare services, previously financed from maternal and child health.
[f] Reflects proposed legislation in 1971 providing reductions of $106 million for elimination of outmoded or duplicative benefits.
Note: Figures may not add to totals because of rounding.

Source: Edited excerpts from The Budget, FY 1971, pp. 164, 171.

members of the population (the major exceptions are those
covered under other Federal retirement plans shown in the
other line items of this subfunction). Although other programs
were established by the Social Security Act (e. g. , unemployment insurance, aid to dependent children), the OASDI program
is the one generally referred to as "Social Security. "

The other two retirement items covered under this subfunction are special retirement and income replacement programs, which were established separately from the social
security system. The Civil Service Retirement System was
set up in 1930, prior to passage of the Social Security Act, and
remains separate from it. Private railroad retirement benefits were consolidated into a program to be administered by the
Government in 1934. Although the Supreme Court invalidated
the initial law, subsequent laws were passed, and the system
was established at about the same time as Social Security and
is now coordinated with it.

The unemployment insurance program was one part of the
Social Security Act of 1935. The program was designed as a
countercyclic measure to keep buying power up during times
of recession or high unemployment and, also, as an aid to
individual worker security. A Federal payroll tax of 3 percent
was assessed on all employers covered under the act, but if
a state program were established, the employer would pay
only 0. 3 percent to the Federal Government, plus whatever tax
the state levied. This left very little choice to the states about
whether to establish a program, but gave them discretion as to
its level and form. It put pressure on them (from employers)
to keep rates low, since the employer paid only the 0. 3 percent
tax to the Federal Government as long as a state program existed, even if the state tax were only 1 percent. Suggestions
have long been made to cover more workers, standardize
benefits, and establish them at a certain percentage of lost
salary, but, at this time, no major moves in this direction
have been implemented. Also included in this line item are a
few Federally funded unemployment compensation programs
for some Federal workers and ex-servicemen.

PUBLIC ASSISTANCE

The largest program under this subfunction is grants to
states for public assistance. This program was established
under the 1935 Social Security Act and is operated through
state and local Government agencies for the benefit of various

groups of people without adequate incomes, which includes
the aged, blind or disabled persons, and families with dependent children. As OASDI benefits increase, the number
of aged included in the public assistance program will decrease, but costs for the disabled and families with children
are increasing. This is probably the most controversial of
all the programs provided for under the Social Security Act,
and bears the brunt of criticism--both conservative and liberal--
of welfare programs.

Major changes in public assistance have been proposed by
the Nixon Administration, and it is likely that the next decade
will be a time of implementation of many of the present suggestions. President Nixon has proposed a Family Assistance
Program to replace the Aid to Families with Dependent Children (ADC) program. Under this program, a family of four
would receive a minimum of $1,600 a year from the Federal
Government, to be supplemented by the states in those states
that presently are above this level. A working head of house-
hold would be able to continue to receive the payments until
his income reached about $4,000 a year. More important than
the specific level of Federal payments, which many have criticized as inadequate, is the concept of minimum national standards and the acceptance by the Federal Government of a larger
responsibility for welfare payments. These trends will probably be strengthened in the 1970's.

The other major area under the public assistance subfunction is food and nutrition programs, of which the largest
is the food stamp program. This program is designed to increase the purchasing power of poor people by providing them
with food stamps, which can be purchased at a subsidized rate
and used to buy food. Nutrition programs for school children
are included in this subfunction.

SOCIAL AND INDIVIDUAL SERVICES

Included under social and individual services are a number
of programs designed to provide aid in nonmonetary ways,
many as supplements to monetary aid. Grants to states for
social services are made in connection with the grants for
public assistance.

Vocational rehabilitation is part of this subfunction. It
is designed to help physically or mentally disabled persons
enter the labor market. Initially begun under the Vocational

Rehabilitation Act of 1920, the program has been expanded
from such services as job training, guidance and counseling,
placement, and provision of artificial limbs. It now includes,
in addition to the services mentioned above, aspects of actual
reduction of disabilities, recovery from psychiatric handicaps,
and services for the "disadvantaged" as well as the disabled.

Other smaller programs under social and individual services include programs of disaster relief; programs for the
aging and for juvenile delinquency; and research, demonstration, and training related to the totality of income security
and welfare programs administered by HEW. The research
element is discussed more fully below.

INCOME SECURITY FOR VETERANS

Because the various subfunctions included under the
veterans field as listed in The Budget seemed to fit well under
other fields, they have been divided among four other fields.
In the Income Security and Welfare field are income security
programs for veterans, such as compensation, pensions, and
insurance programs, and a miscellaneous group of "other
veterans benefits and services," largely made up of administrative expenses for the VA, of which the income security
programs are the major part.

Benefits for veterans go back to the Revolutionary War
and are almost as much a firm commitment of the Government
as is the National Security function, which produces veterans.
Programs treated under this subfunction are almost exclusively the responsibility of the VA, which was created in 1930 to
administer the various programs.

The two largest line items under income security are
service-connected compensation and nonservice-connected
pensions. Service-connected compensation is related to outlays for injuries, diseases, and deaths attributable to military
service. Payments are related to degree of disability and effect on earning power. Payments are made whether the injury
or death occurred in wartime or peacetime, with wartime-
related injuries having higher compensation rates. Payments
include more veterans from Vietnam each year, but veterans
from previous wars are declining. The distinction between
compensation and pensions was established to separate service-
connected hardship from nonservice-connected hardship. Thus,
nonservice-connected pensions may be paid in medical or

economic situations similar to the above program, but, in these cases, the situation is not directly related to an injury incurred during military service. To qualify for benefits under this category, a person must have served during wartime.

The veterans income security subfunction accounts for about 10 percent of 1971 outlays under the total field. Of the other subfunctions, retirement and social insurance is about 75 percent, public assistance about 13 percent, and social and individual services, 3 percent.

RESEARCH AND DEVELOPMENT

Because most of the expenditures in the field of Income Security and Welfare are cash transfers, with disposition controlled by the recipient, R&D in the field is limited, although it has grown by more than 400 percent in the last decade. The R&D conduct figures shown in Table 3 in Chapter 2 are all under the Social and Rehabilitation Service in HEW. Although this field spends slightly more on R&D than a few other fields in absolute dollar terms, as a percent of total outlays, it is the lowest, with only 0.01 percent of total outlays going to R&D conduct in 1971.

R&D programs in the social and rehabilitation service are conducted in mental retardation, maternal and child health, programs for the aging, and rehabilitation research and training. Studies have increased recently that are related to income maintenance and planning and delivery of social services.

NOTES

1. Congressional Quarterly Service, Congress and the Nation (Washington, D.C.: Congressional Quarterly, Inc., 1965), p. 1225.

CHAPTER **5** HEALTH

THE FIELD AS A WHOLE

The functional field of Health includes programs designed
to improve the prevention--and methods of diagnosis and treat-
ment--of adverse health conditions. Included under Health,
for purposes of this discussion, is the functional field of
Health in The Budget, the subfunction entitled "Hospital and
Medical Care" from the veterans functional field in The Budget,
and the AEC Biology and Medicine program. Transferred out
of Health and into the Environment field are efforts aimed at
controlling environmental problems and environmental health
sciences.

Concern of the Federal Government for health problems
emerged as early as 1798, with the establishment of the United
States Marine Hospital Service to care for sick and injured
seamen. This concern was less related to interest in an individual's health than it was to a desire to keep our merchant
marine strong, both for economic and military purposes. A
1963 publication of the Public Health Service (PHS) states that
"since that time, the concept has prevailed that where national
health needs are not being met elsewhere--because of the com-
plexity of the problems, or the insistence of the need, or the
magnitude of the resources required--the Federal Government
has an obligation to help."[1] Some might have questioned this
statement, and some still might do so, even after the multitude
of recent legislative actions with respect to health. However,
it is now certainly a more widely accepted concept of the
Government's role than it was ten or twenty years ago.

Of the three supergoals discussed in Chapter 1, the Health
field contributes primarily to Public Welfare. It has indirect
connections with Economic Growth (a person with good health
is a more productive person) and National Security (the origins
of PHS in caring for merchant marine seamen is a good example), but better health is predominantly related to benefiting
individuals. Partly because of this, partly because of a strong

tradition of individual or family responsibility in caring for
the health of its members, and partly because of the doctor/
patient care for fee system, the Federal role in health activities
has been surrounded by controversy.

A look at the record of legislation in this field indicates
that a major change in the assumption of an expanded role by
the Federal Government came in the 1960's, with implications
of greatly expanding costs and responsibilities in the future.
After the inauguration of President Kennedy, there was a
special message to Congress on "Health" almost every year
of the 1960's. The previous administration had campaigned
in 1952 on a platform that "oppose[d] Federal compulsory
health insurance with its crushing cost, wasteful inefficiency,
bureaucratic dead weight, and debased standards of medical
care".[2] A measure of the change in this philosophy could be
seen in the 1968 Republican platform, which, while stressing
the "traditional patient-doctor relationship," also stated that
"no American should be denied adequate medical treatment."[3]

The change in the national concept of the Government's
role in the field of Health is reflected quite clearly in the data
of Table 2 in Chapter 2. In percent of total Government outlays over the 1961-71 period, Health grew from 2 percent to
9 percent of total, a jump of almost 7 percent, and by far the
largest percentage increase for any field. This increase in
percent of total was the result of an outlay increase from just
under $2 billion in 1961 to almost $17 billion in 1971. A glance
at Table 2 shows the big point of departure to be between 1966
and 1967, when the full effect of the Medicare and Medicaid
programs began to be felt--outlays were more than doubled in
one year. In relative priorities with other functional fields,
Health ranked eighth (out of twelve) in 1961 and third in 1971.
It was one of three fields that grew more than $10 billion during
the period (National Security and Income Security and Welfare
were the others), and one of four that grew by 500 percent or
more (Space, Housing and Community Development, and Environment were the others).

The R&D conduct expenditure data show that health research in 1961 was not in the same controversial position as
health care. R&D expenditures for Health placed the field in
fifth position in 1961 and third in 1971. Health R&D accounted
for 4.5 percent of all R&D expenditures in 1961 and grew to
8.3 percent in 1971, which reflected a growth in funds from
$400 million to $1.2 billion. Because health research was
accepted before health care as being a proper Federal function,
R&D was a high percent of the field's outlays in 1961 (20

percent). By 1971, because of the spectacular rise in outlays
for Health care, R&D funds accounted for a lower percent (8
percent) of total Health functional field outlays.

A more detailed look at overall outlays for Health appears
in Table 10, which shows the actual 1969, and estimated 1970
and 1971, outlays, as given in The Budget, FY 1971. Three
subfunctions (providing or financing medical services, prevention and control of health problems, and development of health
resources) are managed by HEW, with the exception of the
AEC biology and medicine program. The subfunction of
veterans hospital and medical care is administered by the VA.
Other agencies contribute to Health, such as DOD (e. g.,
malaria control), but such activities have been left in the functional field to which the broader program area contributes.
The 1971 distribution by subfunction is 73 percent for medical
services, 3 percent for health problems, 11 percent for veterans, and 14 percent for health services.

PROVIDING OR FINANCING MEDICAL SERVICES

The Medicare and Medicaid programs comprise most of
this subfunction, which is, itself, more than 70 percent of all
Health outlays. Other programs cover services to mothers
and children, family planning, insurance programs for Federal
employees, and some direct medical services.

Medicare

Medicare is the largest component of Health outlays,
making up over 50 percent of 1971 outlays, and is responsible
for the major increases that have taken place in Health outlays
over the 1961-71 period. Established in 1965, Medicare was
the culmination of a debate that had been waged since World
War II over health care for the aged. As authorized, the law
provides for two health insurance programs for those sixty-
five and over: one compulsory and financed under the Social
Security system by means of payroll deductions to cover hospital and nursing home care and the second, a voluntary one,
which includes payment of doctors' bills, to be financed partly
by monthly premiums for those joining and partly from general
revenues.

TABLE 10

Health Outlay Details, FY's 1969-71[a]
(In Millions of Dollars)

Program or Agency	Outlays		
	1969[b]	1970[c]	1971[c]
Providing or Financing Medical Services (HEW):			
Providing Medical Services in HEW Facilities	198	220	235
Financing Medical Services[d]	(9,117)	(10,362)	(11,871)
Medicare (Trust Funds)	6,598	7,538	8,774
Proposed Legislation (Increased Receipts)	---	---	---
Medicaid	2,285	2,612	3,071
Proposed Legislation	---	---	-215
Special Services to Mothers and Children	251	223	241
Proposed Family Planning Legislation	---	---	4
Health Insurance for Federal Employees	-17	-11	-4
Subtotal, Providing or Financing Medical Services	9,315	10,582	12,106
Prevention and Control of Health Problems (HEW):			
Preventing and Controlling Diseases	278	309	345
Protecting the Consumer (Food and Drug Administration)	61	71	85
Other	13	15	19
Subtotal, Prevention and Control of Health Problems	352	396	449
Veterans Hospital and Medical Care (VA):			
Medical Care and Hospital Services	1,451	1,631	1,697
Construction of Hospital and Extended Care Facilities	48	79	58
Medical Administration, Research, and Other[e]	66	78	81
Proposed Legislation[f]	---	---	-40
Subtotal, Veterans Hospital and Medical Care	1,565	1,788	1,796
Development of Health Resources:			
Supporting Biomedical Research (HEW)	1,127	1,190	1,203
Training Health Manpower (HEW)	369	467	535
Constructing Health Facilities (HEW)	292	312	305
Improving the Organization and Delivery of Health Services (HEW)	111	155	172
Biology and Medicine (AEC)	89	89	88
Subtotal, Development of Health Resources	1,988	2,213	2,303
Deductions for Offsetting Receipts:			
Proprietary Receipts from the Public	-2	-1	-1
Total	13,219	14,977	16,652

[a] Includes programs of the Department of Health, Education, and Welfare and the Federal Employees Health Benefits program. Excludes several major health programs that are classified in other functional sections of the budget, notably those of the Office of Economic Opportunity and the Department of Defense.
[b] Actual.
[c] Estimate.
[d] Entries net of intragovernmental transactions: 1969, $1,755 million; 1970, $1,566 million; 1971, $2,135 million.
[e] Includes both Federal funds and trust funds.
[f] Reflects proposed legislation in 1971 providing $40 million in medical care insurance reimbursements.
Note: Figures may not add to totals because of rounding.

Source: Edited excerpts from The Budget, FY 1971, pp. 151 and 171.

Medicaid

Second in expenditures after Medicare, the Medicaid program provides matching grants to states for medical assistance to the poor, no matter what their age. Medicaid originated in the Social Security Amendments Act of 1965 (which established Medicare), and combined some provisions of the Social Security Act, while adding the provision that covered not only older people but also people of any age covered by public assistance programs for the blind, disabled, and dependent children. An additional category was added for the medically needy, who were not quite poor enough to qualify for public assistance.

Other Medical Services

Included under other medical services is maternal and child health, which originated in the Social Security Act of 1935 and provides matching grants to states to fund services for pregnant women and for children. Emphasis is on reduction of deaths, reduction of early childhood health problems, and family planning. A goal has been established of providing family planning services to 5 million women by the middle of the decade. Also under other medical services, direct health care is provided by the Government for a few special groups of the population, such as Indians and merchant seamen.

PREVENTION AND CONTROL
OF HEALTH PROBLEMS

Programs included under the line item "preventing and controlling diseases" are under the Health Services and Mental Health Administration. They include areas such as mental health centers, alcohol and drug programs, public education, health centers and services, regional programs, communicable diseases, and chronic diseases.

Under consumer protection, the Food and Drug Administration (FDA) is responsible for the safety, purity, effectiveness, and labeling of various consumer products.

VETERANS HOSPITAL AND MEDICAL CARE

Over 90 percent of 1971 expenditures for this subfunction are for medical care and hospital services to veterans in VA hospitals and clinics. This care is available to all veterans with service-connected disabilities and to those with nonservice-connected disabilities when they cannot afford other care and when room is available in VA hospitals. The remaining 1971 expenditures are for facility construction, medical administration, research, and other. The research program is described under Health research. Veterans hospital and medical care accounted for 11 percent of Health expenditures in 1971.

DEVELOPMENT OF HEALTH RESOURCES

The development of health resources includes activities related to manpower, facilities, improvement of organization and delivery of services, and R&D.

Health Manpower

Great attention has been focused lately on the lack of adequate numbers of trained medical manpower, from doctors to nurses' aides. Public health and nurse traineeship programs were authorized in 1956 and extended in 1959, and a $1-million annual subsidy to public health schools was instituted in 1958. But it was not until the 1960's that aid for medical manpower expanded greatly. In 1963, Congress authorized aid for medical schools and students and, in 1964, passed the Nurse Training Act. The Allied Health Professions Act of 1966 was designed to provide improved training for allied health professions personnel, such as medical technicians, and to encourage medical people to practice in low-income rural areas. Under a 1966 reorganization plan for the Public Health Service, a separate Bureau of Health Manpower was established to develop and coordinate programs aimed at providing more and better health services personnel.

Health Facilities

Medical facilities, as educational facilities, were an accepted part of Government funding before many other elements of the Health or Education fields. Legislation to support hospital construction was passed just after World War II (the Hill-Burton Act), and it has been extended and expanded since then to include special health facilities other than hospitals and to authorize the making of loans and grants. Grants for health research facilities were authorized by the 1956 Health Research Facilities Act.

Organization and Delivery of Health Services

The demand for health services has risen as the population has grown and as incomes have increased. Coupled with this has been increasing demand for, and more general acceptance of, the philosophy that every citizen, regardless of income, should have access to adequate medical care. The Government has been under pressure, in addition, to "pass on the benefits" of the large research programs to the general public in the form of better health care. Three major programs are included in this category: first, the National Center for Health Services R&D (to use resources more effectively); second, Partnership for Health (grants to states for health planning); and, finally, regional medical programs (to strengthen health resources in a region).

RESEARCH AND DEVELOPMENT

The importance of research in the field of Health has been discussed previously, based on the data presented in Chapter 2. More complete data are presented in Table 11, which follows. Note that these tables include Health R&D funded by the VA and AEC as well as by HEW, although HEW predominates with 88 percent of Health R&D in 1971. It has been noted that Health R&D as a percent of total Health outlays is a much lower percent in 1971 than in 1961. This happened because other activities grew at a faster rate than R&D, not because R&D did not grow. Table 4 in Chapter 2 shows that R&D conduct expenditures grew by over 200 percent over the 1961 to 1971 period. Over the same period, total outlays grew by over 700 percent.

TABLE 11

Health R&D Conduct Expenditures
by Program Area, FY's 1969-71
(In Millions of Dollars)

| Program Area | Agency | R&D Conduct Expenditures | | |
		1969[a]	1970[b]	1971[b]
National Institutes of Health	HEW	834.7	863.8	885.2
Health Services and Mental Health Administration	HEW	139.1	172.5	185.9
Biology and Medicine	AEC	86.0	87.0	86.0
Medical Research	VA	48.0	55.0	56.0
Prosthetic Research	VA	1.3	1.7	2.4
Food and Drug Administration	HEW	7.6	18.6	25.2
Total		1,116.7	1,198.6	1,240.7

[a] Actual.
[b] Estimate.

Source: Data obtained from The Budget, FY 1971, The Department of Health, Education, and Welfare and from the Veterans Administration.

National Institutes of Health (HEW)*

NIH is the primary arm of the U. S. Government in the support of biomedical research, education, and communications. It consists of the National Cancer Institute, National Heart and Lung Institute, National Institute of Dental Research, National Institute of Arthritis and Metabolic Diseases, National Institute of Neurological Diseases and Stroke, National Institute of Allergy and Infectious Diseases, National Institute of General Medical Sciences, National Institute of Child Health and Human Development, National Eye Institute, Division of Research Resources, and National Library of Medicine.

Health Services and Mental Health Administration (HEW)

R&D is carried on in areas related to health services, mental health, and various community health programs. Health services R&D is concerned with improving the organization, delivery, and financing of health services. Mental health R&D efforts include behavioral, clinical, psychopharmacology, and applied research in mental illness and health. Community health R&D focuses on prevention, laboratory diagnosis, and treatment of communicable diseases at the community level.

Food and Drug Administration

The FDA, a part of HEW, conducts research concerning foods, drugs, pesticides, and cosmetics, and on related hazardous substances. Regulations are developed and promulgated for pesticide tolerances and exemptions, food additives, color additives, and food standards. Scientific evaluations are made on the subjects of the regulations and the labeling of hazardous substances. Methods and bases for evaluation of petitions and tolerances are developed and studied.

_____

*Descriptions of the R&D program areas are exerpted from The Budget.

Veterans Administration

The VA medical research program is devoted to patient care and improved diagnostic and treatment procedures. Prosthetic research develops and tests prosthetic, orthopedic, and sensory aids for the purpose of improving care and rehabilitation of disabled veterans, including amputees, paraplegics, and the blind.

Biology and Medicine (AEC)

Research is conducted on the effects of radiation on living organisms and on the environment, protection against the injurious effects of radiation, and development of methods for using radioactive materials in the diagnosis, treatment, and understanding of human diseases, such as cancer. This program includes the measurement and effects of radioactivity (including fallout) in the atmosphere, soils, and oceans for the establishment of standards to insure that AEC activities are conducted safely. The program is coordinated with other Government agencies conducting programs in related aspects of biomedical research.

NOTES

1. U.S. Department of Health, Education, and Welfare, The Public Health Service, Background Material Concerning the Mission and Organization of the Public Health Service (Washington, D.C.: U.S. Government Printing Office, 1963), p. 13.

2. Republican Party Platform (Washington, D.C.: Republican National Committee, 1962).

3. Republican Party Platform (Washington, D.C.: Republican National Committee, 1968).

CHAPTER **6** EDUCATION, KNOWLEDGE, AND MANPOWER

THE FIELD AS A WHOLE

The functional field of Education, Knowledge, and Manpower includes programs designed to improve instruction at academic institutions, to enable individuals to take advantage of such instruction, and to provide a job opportunity for everyone willing to work. Another major part of this category is programs designed to generate fundamental knowledge. The functional field, called "Education and Manpower" in The Budget, has been changed in the title here to include "Knowledge" (although the NSF basic research programs, which this is designed to cover, were already included in the Education and Manpower field in The Budget).

A few elements from other functional fields in The Budget have been moved here. "Scientific investigations in space" has been placed in this category because its objectives are to increase fundamental knowledge of the earth, interplanetary space, the moon, the sun, the solar system, other stars and galaxies, and the effects of the space environment on living organisms. AEC physical research has been included under basic research because it, too, is designed to contribute to fundamental knowledge. Another item included here is "Education Training and Rehabilitation" from the VA, which The Budget included under the Veterans functional field. There are other programs that have not been placed in this functional field, which, nonetheless, have a significant educational component (e. g., DOD educational programs, NASA university programs, and agricultural extension services of the Department of Agriculture). These programs, however, are generally using education efforts for achieving aims more properly a part of another functional field and are, therefore, included in the field to which they are more directly related.

The Federal role in education has, at times, been a topic of acrimonious debate since World War II, but the interest of

65

the Federal Government in this area of public concern goes back even before the Constitution was adopted. In the North-west Ordinance of 1787, it was declared: "Religion, morality, and knowledge being necessary to good government and the happiness of mankind, schools and the means of education shall forever be encouraged."[1] In 1862, the Morrill Act pro-vided land grants to the states for colleges specializing in agriculture and mechanical arts. In 1890, a second Morrill Act provided grants for the operation of these colleges. A Federal Office of Education was established by Congress in 1867

> for the purpose of collecting such statistics and facts as shall show the condition and progress of education in the several states and territories, and of diffusing such information respecting the organization and management of schools and school systems, and methods of teaching, as shall aid the people of the United States in the establishment and maintenance of efficient school systems, and otherwise promote the cause of education throughout the country.[2]

Other landmarks in education were Federal grants-in-aid for vocational education under the Smith-Hughes Act of 1917, emergency aid during the depression, aid to areas "impacted" by tax-free Federal installations beginning in World War II, and the GI Bill of Rights of 1944 (and subsequent extensions), providing benefits for veterans, which greatly expanded the Government's expenditures for education.

These measures were taken against a backdrop of strong and fairly universal agreement that education was, and should be, largely a matter of state and local concern and control. Events in this century, and, especially, since World War II, have served to blunt this feeling somewhat, at least with respect to the question of "concern." It became evident during the draft calls of both World War I and World War II that the public education system, as then constituted, was not providing minimally acceptable education for many people, as evidenced by the high rejection rate because of illiteracy. World War II was also a turning point in the realization of the importance of new knowledge, engendered by research, to the national secur-ity of the United States. In addition to strong growth of R&D in DOD, the NSF was established in 1950 to promote scientific research, coordinate Government research activities and policies, disseminate information, and improve science

teaching. The influence of national security requirements on
the Federal role in education is clear, although it should be
noted that a bill, such as the GI Bill of Rights, was passed
not to provide educated manpower for World War II but to
help in the transition of veterans back into the economy and to
compensate them for wartime service. In 1958, national
security and international competition once again influenced
the Government to undertake additional programs in education;
this time, through passage of the National Defense Education
Act (NDEA), a response to the 1957 orbiting by the U.S.S.R.
of an earth satellite.

Two issues of national policy that came to a head in the
field of education and slowed Federal involvement--even as
new programs were being advocated--were the issues of
racial segregation and of separation of church and state. The
1954 Supreme Court decision that separate schools were in-
herently unequal was a signal of future tumult over education.
The question of public aid to private (especially parochial)
schools was also a topic of strong debate, with fear for the
traditional separation of church and state principle being set
against feelings of discrimination on the part of many Catholics,
whose schools provided over 10 percent of elementary education
and who, in addition, supported public schools through their
taxes. These two issues gradually diminished as "absolutes,"
and both integration and some aid to nonpublic schools are now
accepted principles of the Federal Government in its aid-to-
education programs, although still the subject of much controversy.

Major breakthroughs in Federal aid-to-education came
in 1965, with passage of the Higher Education Act of 1965 and
the Elementary-Secondary Education Act of 1965, termed by
many as the first real "general aids" to education. These
two acts and other more recent legislation and programs will
be discussed in individual subsections later in this chapter.

Closely allied to education and knowledge are the manpower policies of our Government. The 1970 Manpower Report
of the President[3] points out that manpower policies and programs can make special contributions to economic stability
and growth. They can reduce inflationary pressures, increase
worker productivity, increase employment, and help with
special problems of individuals and groups.

Manpower program objectives are discussed under such
headings as employment and unemployment, employment and
poverty income maintenance and work incentives, and equal
employment opportunity. Prior to the 1960's, manpower

activities dealt largely with regulatory areas, such as labor-management relations (Wagner Act of 1935, Taft-Hartley Act of 1947), and wage and hour legislation (e. g. , Fair Labor Standards Act of 1938).

Although the Employment Act of 1946 established the goal of a job for everyone willing to work, this was interpreted primarily in the sense of assuring economic conditions such that jobs were available, with little emphasis on the match between jobs and the labor available. As fears increased in the 1950's over the effects of automation and other types of labor displacement, greater interest grew in matching jobs and people. In the 1960's, which began with high unemployment at the same time that job openings existed, the Government began to take a much more active role in education and training of those who did not qualify for available job openings. Large numbers of people were so poorly educated or lacking in skills that they could not fill the requirements of entry level jobs. A large part of this was attributable to the great influx of relatively undereducated and unskilled people during the 1950's from areas of rural farming. In the 1960's, a series of active manpower training programs was initiated, under both the Labor Department and the OEO.

Of the major national purposes or supergoals reviewed in Chapter 1, the functional field of Education, Knowledge, and Manpower contributes most directly to Public Welfare and Economic Development. This is true, despite the influence of national security needs in stimulating an increased Federal role during and after World War II. The contribution of Education, Knowledge, and Manpower to the Public Welfare is expressed in the statement, quoted earlier, from the Northwest Ordinance of 1787:   "[They are] necessary to good government and the happiness of mankind . . . "[4] An educated populace is one of the underlying assumptions of a form of government that is based on citizen participation and control. An educated labor force has also been recognized more recently as a prime factor in economic growth and social progress in a highly industrialized--or postindustrialized--society. A highly technological society requires a well-educated population, and as science and technology make industry both more complicated and less in need of unskilled labor, education and manpower training must provide a basis for adaptability to changing roles and occupations and for occupations less based on manual skills and more on analytical, service, and managerial skills. Thus, education has an important role in economic growth.

Table 2 in Chapter 2 shows Federal outlays for the field

from 1961 to 1971 and the percent of total for each year. The highest percent is 5.4 percent in 1971, and the movement has been fairly consistently upward from the 2.5 percent of 1961. The largest dollar increases were in 1966 (almost $2 billion), 1967 ($1 billion), and 1970 ($1 billion), as the two major acts of 1965 took effect. The increase between 1961 and 1971 was 3 percent of total Government outlays. In comparison with other fields, Education, Knowledge, and Manpower ranked seventh in 1961, with $2.3 billion, and rose to fourth in 1971, with $10.1 billion, or a growth of more than 300 percent during the period.

From the standpoint of R&D, the field of Education, Knowledge, and Manpower is also in a strong position relative to many other fields, being fourth in rank in 1971. The difference here is that it has been consistently strong in the time period covered (it ranked third in 1961) in contrast to the overall field, which grew in relative importance over the decade. This is due to the fact that the R&D in this field is for the most part more directly related to "Knowledge" than "Education" or "Manpower," and acceptance of large-scale Federal funding for knowledge was achieved before acceptance of large-scale funding for education, with the exception of the post-World War II GI Bill, whose major effect was in an earlier period. A corollary of the increase in aid to education, largely of a non-research nature, has been a decrease in the importance of R&D to the field (as measured by percent of total outlays). R&D was 19 percent of all outlays in this field in 1961 and was down to 12 percent in 1971. Despite this change, R&D is still of greater importance to this field than to most other fields, outranked only by Space, Natural Resources, and Environment. This comparison, and the dollar growth of R&D over the period, are probably more useful in assessing the importance of R&D than the change in the R&D percent of total field outlays. The contrast does, however, indicate that the major growth has come in areas other than R&D. Discussion of the makeup of R&D in the field is contained in a later section.

A more detailed look at total expenditures in this field appears in Table 12, which shows the actual 1969, and estimated 1970 and 1971, outlays as given in The Budget, broken down according to subfunctions and line items under these subfunctions.

HEW (through the Office of Education) has responsibility for about $4 billion of the 1971 outlays appearing on this table. The Labor Department administers over $2 billion and the VA over $1 billion. OEO, NSF, NASA, Interior, and AEC also have major responsibilities in this field. Total outlays for 1971 by major agency are presented in Table 13 below.

TABLE 12

Education, Knowledge, and Manpower Outlay Details,
FY's 1969-71
(In Millions of Dollars)

Program or Agency	Outlays		
	1969[a]	1970[b]	1971[b]
Elementary and Secondary Education:			
Early Childhood Development	350	324	327
Children from Low-Income Families	1,092	1,200	1,324
Education of Handicapped Children	56	75	84
Indian Education (Department of the Interior)	176	229	257
Formula Grants to States	322	209	173
Assistance to Schools in Federally Impacted Areas	398	397	128
Proposed Legislation	---	---	212
Other	86	234	205
Higher Education:			
Student Grants, Direct Loans, and Guaranteed Loans	418	582	632
Construction of Facilities	596	643	580
Other	216	170	237
Vocational Education	262	266	329
Science Education and Basic Research:			
National Science Foundation (NSF)[c]	490	490	490
Space Sciences (NASA)	456	479	451
Physical Research (AEC)	274	278	274
Veterans Education, Training, and Rehabilitation:			
Readjustment Benefits	681	950	1,091
Other	20	26	27
Proposed Legislation [d]	---	25	90
Other Education Aids:			
Educational R&D	85	94	100
Library of Congress and Smithsonian Institution[c]	97	109	112
National Foundation on the Arts and the Humanities	12	23	40
Corporation for Public Broadcasting	5	15	22
Other	174	193	137
Manpower Training:			
Proposed Legislation (Additional First-Year Cost)	---	---	25
On-the-Job Training	121	216	397
Institutional Training	456	384	404
Work Experience	356	357	377
Special Targeting	173	327	411
Program Direction and Research	87	84	106
Other Manpower Aids:			
Federal-State Employment Security Program[c]	630	711	769
Other Manpower Programs[c]	181	217	264
Deductions for Offsetting Receipts:			
Proprietary Receipts from the Public	-13	-13	-14
Total	8,256	9,295	10,060

[a] Actual.
[b] Estimate.
[c] Includes both Federal funds and trust funds.
[d] Reflects proposed legislation to increase GI bill allowance.
Note: Figures may not add to totals because of rounding.

Source: Edited excerpts from The Budget, FY 1971, pp. 138 and 171.

TABLE 13

Education, Knowledge, and Manpower Outlays by Agency,
FY 1971
(In Millions of Dollars)

Agency	Dollars	Percent of Total
Health, Education, and Welfare (Office of Education)	4,135	41.0
Labor	2,240	22.2
Veterans Administration	1,208	12.0
Office of Economic Opportunity	574	5.7
National Science Foundation	490	4.9
National Aeronautics and Space Administration	451	4.5
Department of the Interior	311	3.1
Atomic Energy Commission	274	2.7
Housing and Urban Development	150	1.5
Legislative Branch	57	0.6
Smithsonian Institution	55	0.5
National Foundation on Arts and Humanities	40	0.4
National Labor Relations Board	37	0.4
Corporation for Public Broadcasting	22	0.2
Equal Employment Opportunity Commission	18	0.2
Federal Mediation and Conciliation Service	10	0.1
Other	4	0.1[a]
	10,074	100.0
Receipts from the Public	-14	
Total Outlays	10,060	

[a] Figure is rounded.
Note: Figures may not add to totals because of rounding.

Source: Data compiled from The Budget, FY 1971, Table 14, pp. 571-583.

71

ELEMENTARY AND SECONDARY EDUCATION[*]

The Elementary and Secondary Education Act of 1965 was the first legislation providing general aid to schools at this level, concentrating on aid on the basis of number of children from low-income families rather than to schools as such. Because of this indirect approach and, also, because of the loosening up in the public/private school controversy, the bill passed. The bill had five titles providing for five major programs:

1.   Title I provided for a program to help children from low-income families. School districts could spend funds in any way agreed upon by state and Federal educational agencies, taking into account needs for nonpublic school education.
2.   Title II provided for a program for acquisition of various printed instructional materials, such as library books and textbooks, which were to be available for loan to private schools.
3.   Title III provided for a program for supplementary educational centers and services not provided by individual schools.
4.   Title IV amended Cooperative Research Act of 1954 by providing for a program of grants for research, surveys, and demonstrations in education and for dissemination of information. Provided also for training in educational research and for construction and operation of regional education research centers.
5.   Title V provided for a program to assist states in strengthening their educational agencies.
Three additional titles have subsequently been added:
1.   Title VI provides for assistance to states in educational services for mentally and physically handicapped children.
2.   Title VII provides for educational programs for children from non-English-speaking families.
3.   Title VIII provides grants for programs to prevent school dropouts.
Also included under this subfunction of elementary and secondary education is the Teacher Corps, designed to improve elementary teaching in low-income areas through the use of experienced teachers and intern teams. This program was authorized in 1965 but not funded until late in FY 1966; it has had continuing appropriation problems, never being funded

---

[*]This part of the chapter goes into greater detail in discussing legislation and policy under the subfunctions listed in Table 14.

near the amount requested. Amendments designed to ensure local control have quieted some opposition.

The program of aid to schools in Federally impacted areas goes back to the Lanham Act of 1940, providing aid for areas affected by defense installations or plants. Later legislation has broadened the concept of Federally impacted areas to include Federal facilities and employees generally, and Congress has been consistently more liberal in funding this program than the various Presidents have wished.

HIGHER EDUCATION

Also passed in 1965 was the Higher Education Act of 1965, involving the Federal Government in major new aid programs to institutions of higher education and to students. Undergraduate scholarships and Federally insured loans were made available for the first time, in addition to the already instituted aid for constructing facilities. The Act contained the following titles:

1. Title I established community service programs by colleges and universities, with emphasis on urban and suburban problems; it authorized a Council on Continuing Education.

2. Title II authorized grants to improve library resources at institutions of higher education and for training of librarians and information specialists.

3. Title III provided funds to raise the academic quality of developing institutions and authorized "national teaching fellowships" to bring teachers to these institutions.

4. Title IV authorized Federal scholarships, Federally insured loans, and interest subsidies for college students; work-study programs were transferred from OEO to the Office of Education.

5. Title V established a National Teacher Corps and teacher fellowships.

6. Title VI authorized grants to improve classroom instruction, providing funds for educational laboratory and media equipment and for instructional workshops.

7. Title VII increased funds and liberalized requirements for college and university facilities grants under Higher Education Facilities Act of 1963.

8. Title VIII encouraged the sharing of resources among colleges.

9. Title IX authorized grants for graduate training for careers in governmental services.

10. Title X authorized grants to improve Ph. D. training.
11. Title XI authorized grants for clinical experience for law
students.
12. Title XII contained general provisions and discussion of
absence of Federal control.

VOCATIONAL EDUCATION

Vocational education was first supported by the Federal
Government in 1917 under the Smith-Hughes Act, which became the basis for Government activity in this area until after
World War II. Activities included were limited to the areas
of agriculture, home economics, trade, and industrial subjects.
The first substantial revision, in 1956, included training of
practical nurses and training in the fisheries trades (the latter
was not funded until 1963). In 1958, the National Defense
Education Act expanded the programs to include training in
technical and scientific fields. The 1960's saw further changes
in the character and scope of work-related education programs
through a variety of new laws:
1.   1961 Area Redevelopment Act (ARA), providing job training
in economically depressed areas
2.   1962 Manpower Development and Training Act (MDTA),
providing training for workers with outdated skills
3.   1962 Trade Expansion Act, providing training for workers
who lose jobs because of foreign competition
4.   1962 Public Welfare Amendments, providing training for
people on relief.
These new programs were aimed at specific groups in the
population who were adversely affected by economic and technological conditions, whereas previous vocational education
had been aimed at the general population. In 1963, further
expansion of vocational education emphasized work-study and
residential vocational school programs. In 1965, Congress
passed a bill for loan insurance and interest subsidies for
vocational education that was comparable to these programs
in the higher education bill. Increased attention was given in
1968 legislation to people who were physically handicapped or
economically disadvantaged.

SCIENCE EDUCATION AND BASIC RESEARCH

This subfunction includes the space sciences activities of NASA, the activities of NSF, and the physical research of AEC. These activities are of a somewhat different character from most of the activities discussed above, being more in the "Knowledge" part of this field, and they have not been so involved in the policy questions surrounding the question of Federal aid to education since World War II.

NSF was, in large part, an outgrowth of the World War II realization of the crucial contributions of science to national security and the need for continuing support of research. There was a desire to have the Government support research through a civilian agency as well as through DOD, and, in 1950, Congress established NSF to promote basic scientific research and science education and to establish and coordinate national science policies.

NSF was authorized to make grants and loans for basic research in science and engineering, to award scholarships and fellowships for science education, to perform certain information services and gather information, and to coordinate its research program and other research programs. NSF actually did little in the field of policy formulation and coordination and, in 1962, this function was largely transferred to the White House Office of Science and Technology. With passage of the National Sea Grant College and Program Act of 1966, NSF was authorized to establish programs of research and training in marine resources at institutions of higher education.

The first major revisions in the role of NSF came in 1968, with passage of a law broadening the scope and nature of Foundation activities. The law reaffirms the Foundation's responsibilities for basic research and education, making explicit the implied consent to fund social science activities. Another change is the expansion of support to applied as well as basic research. Other changes include greater participation in international scientific activities, expansion of data collection and analysis functions, and various administrative modifications. The research activities of NSF are covered in the later section on R&D.

The objectives of the space sciences activities of NASA were described earlier, and other information on this research program appear in the R&D section. Discussion of the background and aims of NASA is covered in the chapter on Space. AEC physical research is also described in the R&D section.

VETERANS EDUCATION, TRAINING, AND REHABILITATION

Veterans education originated with the World War II GI Bill of Rights, which was started as a program to help veterans readjust to civilian life and prevent a sudden influx of inadequately trained or educated people into the labor market. The VA paid for tuition and living expenses for up to four years of formal schooling. Korean War veterans could receive similar benefits for three years. In 1966, Congress passed a Cold War GI Bill, which established a permanent program of aid for educational and vocational training and a loan program for men who had served since the termination of the Korean War bill. Such expenditures in the years after World War II were virtually the entire field of Federal aid to education, amounting to billions of dollars.

OTHER EDUCATION AIDS

This subfunction contains a rather diverse group of aids to education, other than those discussed above, including such programs as educational R&D, funds for libraries, and the Smithsonian Institution. Educational R&D was given its first major impetus in 1954, with authorization for the Office of Education to enter into cooperative arrangements with colleges and universities for joint studies of educational problems. Title IV of the Elementary and Secondary Education Act of 1965 expanded educational R&D and authorized grants, included dissemination of information and demonstration projects, and expanded grant and contract recipients beyond colleges and universities. A description of the research program is contained in the R&D section.

The Library of Congress is the national library of the United States, initially established for the Congress but now also available for general use. The Smithsonian Institution was created in 1846 for the "increase and diffusion of knowledge among men." Its activities include research, exploration, and exhibitions of scientific and cultural interest.

The National Foundation on the Arts and Humanities was created, in 1965, to encourage and support national progress in the humanities and the arts. Its program is carried out through grants, consultative services, and stimulation of

private support. The Corporation for Public Broadcasting
sponsors noncommercial television and radio programs.

MANPOWER TRAINING

The subfunction of manpower training is largely the
responsibility of the Labor Department, including several
programs that originated in OEO and have been transferred to
Labor. In addition, some programs are still run by OEO and
by HEW. Further consolidation of statutory authorizations
and decentralization of planning and operation to state and local
governments is proposed by the Nixon Administration's Manpower Training Act.

The major program was established by the Manpower
Development and Training Act of 1962, which authorized vocational and on-the-job training in local Manpower Development
and Training centers, focusing on youth, unemployed heads of
families, and people who had lost their jobs because of technological change. Later changes placed emphasis on training
illiterates and school dropouts who are unemployed.

The next big step came with the Economic Opportunity
Act of 1964, which established OEO and provided for broader
manpower programs, which would include basic educational
components and health and counseling services. Three programs were established in three different agencies--the Job
Corps in OEO, the Neighborhood Youth Corps in Labor, and
work-experience programs in HEW. The Job Corps set up
special training centers, removed from the ghetto areas, for
youth from ages sixteen to twenty-one, most of whom had not
completed high school. Criticized for high costs, discipline
problems, and for the concept of establishing centers away
from the areas where the participants live, the Job Corps has
been transferred to the Labor Department and reduced in size.

The Neighborhood Youth Corps provided work experience
and training in the local areas where the participants lived and
was designed to reach poor people, aged sixteen to twenty-one,
who were still in school, on summer vacation, or who were
unemployed dropouts.

The work-experience program was to enable heads of
families receiving ADC payments to be trained and employed.
This program was superseded by the work-incentive program,
authorized by the Social Security Amendments Act of 1967,
which required adult recipients of ADC payments to participate

in work-training programs and provided a monthly incentive payment. This program is expected to be superceded by the Family Assistance Program under the Nixon's Administration's welfare reform programs.

Other smaller programs were aimed at employing local residents in slum rehabilitation projects, training aids in service fields, such as health and education, and using the unemployed in beautification projects. In an attempt to coordinate the various manpower programs, the Concentrated Employment Program (CEP) was begun in 1967 to coordinate all programs in an area and to recruit, test, and place the unemployed in one of the available programs.

A change of emphasis was initiated in 1967 with a few pilot programs to enlist the help of private business in training of the "hard-core unemployed," a term with a fairly loose definition but which presupposes that many such people are employable with some additional training. The program became full-blown in 1968, with creation of the National Alliance of Businessmen to spearhead a program of business participation in training, called Job Opportunities in the Business Sectors (JOBS). Local alliances were established in major cities to identify and recruit the hard-core unemployed and to obtain hiring and training pledges from local organizations. The objective was to have 500,000 such people working by June, 1971. The Federal Government would assume the burden of training and associated costs above a normal training cost. The hope was that industry would be able to train people for actual positions, which they then would fill. An undetermined question was whether industry would stand to benefit from such a program in terms of worker productivity and profits and, whether, in the absence of such incentives, the "social conscience" motive was one that could be sustained over time. Many have also suggested that tax credits would be more acceptable to industry and create less red tape than the present reimbursement plan. The JOBS program and on-the-job training will be merged under present plans.

OTHER MANPOWER AIDS

The largest part of this subfunction is the Federal-state employment security program in the Labor Department, designed to help people obtain employment and to match jobs with people. The U.S. Employment Service has been revamped to strengthen its services, and it is experimenting with computerized methods in many areas, such as job matching.

Some other smaller programs under "Other Manpower Aids" include:

1. Programs of the Labor Department concerned with wage and labor standards

2. Bureau of Labor Statistics (Labor), which gathers factual data in the field of labor economics

3. Labor-Management Services Administration (Labor), which is responsible for activities related to labor-management relations

4. Bureau of Mines (Interior) health and safety program to improve conditions in the mineral industry

5. National Labor Relations Board, which hears charges of unfair labor practices and conducts secret ballots to determine employee representation

6. Federal Mediation and Conciliation Service, which helps settle labor-management disputes through conciliation and mediation

7. National Mediation Board, which mediates labor-management disputes in railways and airlines and settles employee representation disputes

8. Equal Employment Opportunity Commission, which attempts to end discrimination in employment practices and promotes programs of equal opportunity in jobs.

R&D is an important component of this functional field. R&D comprised 19 percent of all 1961 expenditures for this functional field but was down to 12 percent in 1971, reflecting the increase in aids to education under the 1965 Elementary and Secondary Education Act, the Higher Education Act, and manpower programs under MDTA. This field is outranked only by Space, Natural Resources, and Environment in percentage to R&D. The place of R&D in this field and vis-à-vis other fields was reviewed earlier. Table 14 shows specific R&D program areas and expenditures for 1969 through 1971.

Because of the way subfunctions are set up in this field, the distribution of R&D by subfunction is not as meaningful as in some other fields. The subfunction of science education and basic research is specifically oriented toward research, and it accounts for 86 percent of all R&D in the field in 1971. About 10 percent is under other education aids, which includes educational R&D for the other education subfunctions as well. The manpower subfunction accounts for about 4 percent of the field's R&D.

TABLE 14

Education, Knowledge, and Manpower R&D Conduct
Expenditures by Program Area, FY's 1969-71
(In Millions of Dollars)

1971 Rank	Program Area	Agency	1969[a]	1970[b]	1971[b]
1	Scientific Investigations in Space	NASA	449.9	474.0	445.9
2	Physical Research	AEC	274.0	278.0	274.0
3	Basic Research Grants	NSF	183.3	185.4	188.5
4	Office of Education	HEW	88.1	91.7	95.2
5	Office of Economic Opportunity	OEO	28.3	18.5	37.0
6	National Research Programs	NSF	8.9	18.9	34.9
7	National Research Centers	NSF	22.9	26.9	31.3
8	Institutional Science Programs	NSF	27.4	29.1	24.6
9	Smithsonian Institution		15.6	16.8	19.7
10	Office of Manpower Administration	Labor	12.5	12.4	13.0
11	Program Development and Management	NSF	11.0	12.4	13.0
12	Science Information Activities	NSF	8.5	9.9	10.9
13	National Sea Grant Program	NSF	2.1	4.6	7.1
14	Course Content Improvement	NSF	13.5	9.9	6.3
15	Bureau of Labor Statistics	Labor	3.8	3.8	3.9
16	Planning and Policy Studies	NSF	1.9	2.5	2.7
17	Other Labor	Labor	2.4	2.2	2.6
	Total		1,154.1	1,197.0	1,210.6

[a] Actual.
[b] Estimate.

Source: Compiled from The Budget, FY 1971, and data from individual agencies.

RESEARCH AND DEVELOPMENT*

National Science Foundation

Support of Scientific Research

This program area consists of research project support, specialized research facilities and equipment, national and special research programs, and national research centers. These four programs fund the following:
1.   Scientific research in specialized areas, determined by NSF to require increased support to promote the national interests
2.   Major specialized scientific facilities and equipment, primarily at colleges and universities, required for the conduct of advanced scientific studies
3.   Programs where the magnitude of the effort requires planning and funding on a national basis and in situations where a special research effort is likely to have a beneficial impact on current problems
4.   The development and operation of national research centers to meet national needs for research in specific areas of science requiring facilities, equipment, and operational support beyond the financial capabilities of academic institutions.

Computing Activities in Education and Research

This program area consists of support of projects designed to explore new applications of computers to education and research and to promote experiments in multiinstitutional cooperation in computer utilization.

International Cooperative Scientific Activities

This program provides support for international cooperative research and science education activities.

Institutional Support for Science

This program provides support to develop institutional capabilities for the conduct of advanced scientific research,

---

*Descriptions of the R&D program areas are excerpted from The Budget or from material received from the agency.

as well as the interdisciplinary competence needed to gain a
fundamental understanding of pressing problems and the kinds
and levels of trained manpower necessary for these purposes.

Science Information Services

This program supports the collection, translation, and
dissemination of information on the results of research and
the development of improved methods for the exchange of
scientific information.

Planning and Policy Studies

This program supports surveys and analytical studies of
R&D within the various sectors of the economy and the current
and projected status of scientific manpower and other resources
required for the conduct of scientific activities. These studies
are related to the formulation of long-range national policies
concerning science.

National Sea Grant Program

This program provides support, primarily at academic
institutions, for research education and training and advisory
services aimed at assisting man in the intelligent utilization
of resources of the seas and the development of the resource
potential of the Great Lakes of the United States.

AEC Physical Research

This comprises basic and applied research in the physical
sciences. The Commission serves as the executive agent for
the nation's high energy physics programs. The objective of
thermonuclear plasma research is to determine whether the
energy released by thermonuclear reactions can be controlled
and made useful. This area is expected to expand with the
completion of large new experimental devices and the initiation
of others needed to test recent concepts.

HEW Office of Education

The Office of Education supports a broad range of efforts
to improve education through research and demonstration

centers, development of new curricular materials, and teaching techniques. Emphasis is now being placed on large programmatic efforts to replace many of the smaller, more discrete, efforts of the past. Establishment and operation of regional resource centers to develop and apply methods of appraising the special educational needs of handicapped children are provided for as well as the training of persons in the use of materials for the handicapped. In the area of vocational and adult education, attention is directed toward upgrading vocational education programs, stimulating new ways to create a bridge between school and earning a living for school dropouts and youths graduating from high school who lack employable skills.

Smithsonian Institution

Besides maintaining exhibits, the Smithsonian conducts research in the natural and physical sciences and in the history of cultures, technology, and arts. Attention is being directed to research, information, and education related to environmental problems.

National Aeronautics and Space Administration

Scientific investigations in space increases the knowledge of the earth, interplanetary space, the moon, the sun, the solar system, other stars and galaxies, and the effects of the space environment on living organisms. The flight systems used are sounding rocket probes, orbiting spacecraft, and spacecraft designed for planetary and interplanetary missions.

Department of Labor

The research program of the Department of Labor includes studies of current and prospective manpower requirements and resources, skill requirements and supply, job opportunities and occupational outlook, factors that tend to impede labor mobility, manpower utilization, and occupational training problems of youth. This activity also funds manpower research contracts and administers a program of experimental and demonstration training projects. These efforts are directed toward furthering the objectives of the Manpower Development and Training Act of 1962, as amended. Research within the

Department of Labor is carried out by the Office of Manpower Policy, Evaluation and Research of the Manpower Administration; Bureau of Labor Statistics, and the Wage and Hour and Public Contracts Division of the Wage and Labor Standards Administration.

Office of Economic Opportunity

OEO's research and pilot projects are designed to serve as the basis for planning programs for alleviating poverty and promoting equality of opportunity. This includes identification of need, design of experimental projects, the conduct and evaluation of social experiments, expansion of successful experimental efforts to pilot scale, and development of mechanisms for moving these programs to full-scale operation, either within the agency or to other organizations.

NOTES

1. U.S. Department of Health, Education, and Welfare, Education in the United States of America, Office of Education Report No. OE-10006 (Washington, D.C.: U.S. Government Printing Office, 1960), p. 8.

2. Ibid.

3. Manpower Report of the President (Washington, D.C.: U.S. Government Printing Office, 1970), p. 19.

4. Education in the United States of America, op. cit., p. 8.

7

COMMERCE, TRANSPORTATION, AND COMMUNICATIONS

THE FIELD AS A WHOLE

The functional field of Commerce, Transportation, and Communications includes programs designed to "improve transportation and communication services, assist business, develop depressed areas, and assure effective competition and fair business practices."[1] The Budget categorization has been used for this field with a few exceptions. The Environmental Science Services Administration has been transferred to the Environment field. Aircraft technology from NASA, which The Budget includes under Space, has been brought to this field under the subfunction of air transportation. The only other change is one of retitling; the word "communications" has been added to the title so that it is now "Commerce, Transportation, and Communications," although it is generally referred to by the short form "Commerce."

The necessity for some control over commerce was one of the reasons the Constitution of the United States was written. Under the Articles of Confederation, which served as Federal law between 1781 and 1789, each state was really an independent and sovereign entity, and the Confederation was largely a "league of friendship,"[2] with no real authority to collect revenues or regulate trade. This presented practical difficulties, and a convention of states was proposed by Virginia in 1786 to "consider how far a uniform system in their commercial relations may be necessary to their common interests and their permanent harmony."[3] Because of lack of authority of the delegations, the main result of this meeting was a report, written by Alexander Hamilton, which suggested another convention with enlarged powers, because

> [the] power of regulating trade is of such compre-
> hensive extent, and will enter so far into the
> general System of the Federal Government, that to
> give it efficacy, and to obviate questions and doubts
> concerning its precise nature and limits, may re-
> quire a corresponding adjustment of other parts
> of the Federal System. [4]

The resulting meeting was the Convention of 1787, which produced the Constitution. After taxation, the power to regulate
interstate and foreign commerce was probably the next most
important new power granted in this document.

    In its contribution to the supergoals discussed in Chapter
1, the field of Commerce contributes primarily to the supergoal of Economic Development. Areas would be slowed down
in their development if it were not possible to trade with
other areas, and this necessitates a transport and communications network as well as a means for providing and regulating it. Functions relating to this requirement are primarily
handled by the Department of Transportation and independent
regulatory agencies. The Department of Commerce has major
responsibility for the subfunction entitled "Advancement of
Business," which includes such programs as export promotion,
assisting business, setting physical standards, promoting
technology, and collecting statistics. It also has assumed
responsibility more recently for more generalized help to
business through area and regional development. The Commerce field is also related to the supergoals of National
Security and Public Welfare. Its contribution to National
Security has been the basis for many Government programs
in support of the field.

    The allocation of Government funds to this functional field
over the 1961-71 period shows that it is relatively high in rank
by comparison with most other fields but that its percent of
total outlays has gone down over the 1961-71 period, despite
a rise in the first half of the period. In 1961, Commerce
outlays were 5.5 percent of total Government outlays, as
shown in Table 2. In 1965, this figure was up to 6.6 percent,
but fell quickly thereafter and, for 1971, is estimated to be
4.7 percent of total. This occurred despite an overall rise
in actual dollar outlays and is a result of much larger growth
in other fields. In comparison with other fields, Commerce
ranked third (out of twelve) in 1961 and fifth in 1971.

    In expenditures for R&D, Commerce ranks a little
lower--at just about the midpoint (sixth or seventh out of

twelve)--in 1961 and 1971. Commerce R&D is now 2.8 percent of all Government R&D expenditures. R&D has doubled in importance to the field, from 2.4 percent of total Commerce outlays in 1961 to 4.8 percent in 1971.

A more detailed look at overall outlays for Commerce appears in Table 15, which shows the actual 1969, and estimated 1970 and 1971, outlays as given in The Budget, broken down into subfunctions and line items under these subfunctions.

The estimated 1971 expenditures are shown by agency in Table 16. The Transportation Department has primary responsibility for expenditures in this field, with 77 percent of 1971 expenditures. Commerce is second with 9 percent, and the Post Office third with 4 percent. The remaining 10 percent is allocated among many other agencies and groups, including the independent regulatory agencies.

Because the transportation activities shown are divided into three separate subfunctions, it may be useful in this overall section to provide more general information on transportation policies and programs, since the three subfunctions of air, water, and ground transportation make up such a large portion (82 percent) of the field's outlays. In addition, part of the subfunction "Regulation of Business" pertains to transportation. The Federal Government is deeply involved with the nation's transport systems, and it exercises its powers and influence through promotional and regulatory activities. The governmental role that has evolved in the area of transportation, though greatly changed and expanded over time, derives from the Constitutional provision, discussed earlier, giving the Federal Government authority to regulate interstate commerce. More recent promotional activities have often been associated, at least in theory, with National Defense needs and, also, Economic Development and General Welfare.

In many ways, the usual classification by mode (air, water, and ground), as is done in The Budget, is a necessary approach, because transportation policies and programs have not, to date, been treated on a comprehensive basis but are largely an accumulation of individual policies and programs. President Kennedy, in 1962, characterized transportation policy as "a chaotic patchwork of inconsistent and often obsolete legislation and regulation [which] has evolved from a history of specific actions addressed to specific problems of specific industries at specific times."[5] (This is still generally true, despite the expressed desire to develop a more coordinated national transportation policy that would be competitive among modes, fair in its treatment of various modes,

TABLE 15

Commerce, Transportation, and Communications
Outlay Details, FY's 1969-71
(In Millions of Dollars)

Program or Agency	Outlays		
	1969[a]	1970[b]	1971[b]
Air Transportation:			
Airways and Airports (DOT):			
Present Programs	917	1,087	1,198
Proposed Legislation	---	2	163
Supersonic Transport (DOT)	81	163	275
Air Carrier Subsidies(Civil Aeronautics Board)	44	37	31
Aircraft Technology (NASA)	168	180	184
Water Transportation:			
Merchant Marine Aids (Commerce)	314	319	333
Coast Guard (DOT)	548	593	597
Other	2	7	8
Ground Transportation (DOT):			
Highways[c]	4,255	4,627	4,573
Urban Mass Transportation:			
Present Programs	142	161	204
Proposed Legislation	---	---	80
Railroad and Related Systems	16	21	23
Postal Service (Post Office)	920	1,247	382
Advancement of Business (Commerce and DOT):[d]			
Export and Travel Promotion[c]	22	29	33
Economic and Demographic Statistics[c]	51	165	95
Physical Standards	35	43	43
Promotion of Technology[c]	51	56	57
Small Business Assistance (SBA)	110	273	178
Federal Deposit Insurance Corporation (FDIC)	-313	-333	-359
Other Aids to Business[c]	-35	48	54
Area and Regional Development (Commerce, Interior, and Funds to President):			
Area and District Development	197	255	229
Regional Development[c]	179	277	310
Other	208	185	172
Regulation of Business	107	123	124
Deductions for Offsetting Receipts:			
Interfund and Intragovernmental Transactions	-49	-39	-11
Proprietary Receipts from the Public	-108	-105	-206
Total	7,862	9,423	8,770

[a]Actual.
[b]Estimate.
[c]Includes both Federal funds and trust funds.
[d]Except as noted.
Note: Figures may not add to totals because of rounding.

Source: Edited excerpts from The Budget, FY 1971, p. 116.

TABLE 16

Commerce, Transportation, and Communications
Outlays by Agency, FY 1971
(In Millions of Dollars)

Agency		Dollars	Percent of Total
Transportation		7,155	76.6
Commerce		845	9.0
Post Office (Net After Receipts)		382	4.1
Funds to President (Appalachian Development)		279	3.0
National Aeronautics and Space Administration		184	2.0
Department of the Interior		171	1.8
Civil Aeronautics Board		42	0.4
Small Business Administration		178	1.9
Interstate Commerce Commission		25	0.3
Federal Communications Commission		25	0.3
Securities and Exchange Commission		22	0.2
Federal Trade Commission		21	0.2
Other		18	0.2
		9,346	100.0
Federal Deposit Insurance Corporation[a]	-359		
Adjustments	-217		
	-576	-576	
Total Outlays		8,770	

[a]FDIC, because it had negative expenditures, is not included
  in the percent distribution.

Note: Figures may not add to totals because of rounding.

  Source: Data compiled from The Budget, FY 1971,
Table 14, pp. 571-583.

and in the public interest.) The quote is from a message on
transportation, transmitted to the Congress by President
Kennedy, which was a major attempt to outline his ideas on
transportation policy.   This message expressed the basic objective of the U. S. transportation system as assuring

> the availability of the fast, safe, and economic
> transportation services needed in a growing and
> changing economy to move people and goods, with-
> out waste or discrimination, in response to pri-
> vate and public demands at the lowest cost con-
> sistent with health, convenience, national security
> and other broad public objectives. [6]

Some Federal policy expressions of this objective suggested
in this speech were the following:
1. Less Federal regulation and subsidization in the long run
2. Equal competitive opportunity
3. Free regulated common carriers from outmoded Federal
rules that put them at a disadvantage vis-à-vis private and
exempt carriers
4. The common carrier should remain the core of our transport system
5. No mode should be at a competitive disadvantage with other
modes because of Government subsidies or regulation.
     Although President Kennedy did not, in this message, men-
tion establishing a Cabinet-level Department of Transportation
(DOT), the proposal had been made in the 1961 Doyle Report[7]
and, in 1966, such a department was created. Although this
was regarded as a step toward the possibility of a more coordinated and rational Federal approach to transport policy,
it has been criticized as not vesting enough authority in the
Secretary and, also, because it omits many aspects of Federal
interest in transportation from DOT's purview, such as the
regulatory functions and the Maritime Administration. Nonetheless, the creation of a Transportation Department has
focused attention on the need to think of transportation policies
in a more interdependent way.
     The three subfunctions that deal exclusively with trans-
portation--air, water, and ground--are discussed below, with
the four smaller subfunctions (postal service, advancement of
business, area and regional development, and regulation of
business) after transportation. Regulatory activities relating
to transportation are included under "Regulation of Business."

AIR TRANSPORTATION

Air transportation is largely the responsibility of the Federal Aviation Administration (FAA), which is part of DOT, with NASA and the Civil Aeronautics Board (CAB) playing lesser, but important, roles.

The FAA works under the following policy guides, as expressed in the Federal Aviation Administration Act of 1958:
1. To regulate air commerce in such manner as to best promote its development and safety and fulfill the requirements of national defense
2. To promote, encourage, and develop civil aeronautics
3. To control the use of the navigable airspace of the United States and to regulate both civil and military operations in such airspace in the interest of the safety and efficiency of both
4. To consolidate R&D with respect to air navigation facilities, as well as the installation and operation thereof
5. To develop and operate a common system of air traffic control and navigation for both military and civil aircraft. [8]

The FAA has been involved, over the last few years, in a Government-supported program to develop and build a civil supersonic transport (SST). Because the development costs were regarded as too heavy an investment for private firms to be willing to undertake, the Government is sharing by contributing 90 percent of prototype development costs, under a plan that calls for later repayment from sales. The SST program is the subject of great controversy because of concern over its environmental effects (including noise) and questions regarding transportation priorities.

The aspects of the CAB that are included in this subfunction (see others under "Regulation of Business") are the carrier payments (subsidies).

NASA's responsibilities in air transportation are predominantly in R&D (as is true of other NASA functions), which is aimed at extending the national capability in aeronautics and supporting other Government agencies having interests in this area. In the latter respect, NASA coordinates its R&D with FAA on the civilian side and with DOD on the military side. Because of its primary contribution to National Security, transportation activities of DOD have been included in that functional field.

WATER TRANSPORTATION

Activities under this subfunction are divided, with the Transportation Department predominant because it has responsibility for the Coast Guard. The Commerce Department also has major activities because the Maritime Administration was not transferred to DOT when it was created in 1966.

The Coast Guard is considered a branch of the U. S. Armed Forces and serves as part of the Navy under Presidential directive or in time of war. The Coast Guard is expected to maintain a state of military readiness, even when not serving under the Navy. The principal functions of the Coast Guard, other than military readiness, are search and rescue services, merchant marine safety programs, aids to navigation for both military and civilian commerce, and port security and law enforcement in U. S. waters or on the high seas. The Coast Guard provides oceanographic data as part of its other activities and as part of the overall Government program to further knowledge of the seas.

The Maritime Administration is responsible for the growth and development of the United States merchant marine so that it will be

(a) adequate to carry the Nation's domestic waterborne commerce and a substantial portion of its foreign commerce during peacetime; (b) capable of serving as a naval and military auxiliary in time of war or national emergency; (c) owned and operated under U. S. flag by citizens of the United States, so far as may be practicable; and (d) composed of the best equipped, safest, and most suitable types of ships manned by a trained and efficient citizen personnel. [9]

To meet these objectives, long-standing Government policy has been to subsidize these commercial vessels to keep them competitive with vessels of other nations. Both construction and operating costs for foreign vessels are well below those of the United States. In addition, the Government pays the full cost of certain defense features that are added to enable conversion to military use. Because of the lack of competitive capabilities of our merchant marine and the question of its potential usefulness in modern warfare, some are now challenging the necessity of Government support, while others are challenging its adequacy.

GROUND TRANSPORTATION

This subfunction expends over half of the total outlays for the Commerce functional field and is, almost exclusively, the responsibility of the Federal Highway Administration in DOT. Two other smaller components of this subfunction are the Urban Mass Transportation Administration and the Federal Railroad Administration, both in DOT.

The Federal Highway Administration administers programs of Federally aided highway construction, construction of roads on Federal lands, and research and some safety functions. The programs of Federally aided highway construction, which comprise the major expenditures, are funded through a trust fund made up of user charges and are the responsibility of the Bureau of Public Roads. The trust fund is used to finance 90 percent of state programs that are involved in the 41,000-mile interstate and defense highway system and 50 percent of improvements to other approved roads. Estimated 1971 expenditures from this trust fund are half of the total estimated 1971 outlays for the entire Commerce functional field. The National Highway Safety Bureau, now separate from the Federal Highway Administration, administers programs of highway safety and safety research.

The Urban Mass Transportation Administration was created within DOT in 1968, incorporating programs formerly in the Housing and Urban Development Department (HUD). DOT coordinates with HUD to see that urban transportation fits in with broader urban development.

The Federal Railroad Administration administers programs and policies regarding rail transportation and the High-Speed Ground Transportation program.

POSTAL SERVICE

The Post Office Department expends all funds under this subfunction. The postal service dates to pre-Constitutional times and has been a Cabinet-level department since 1872. Under the Postal Policy Act of 1958, the purpose of the Post Office Department is "to unite more closely the American people, to promote the general welfare, and to advance the national economy."[10] Most activities of the Department are covered by revenues obtained from charges for its services,

and its operating budget is much larger than that shown on
Table 15.   Table 17 shows the Post Office Department total
program.

Major reforms are occurring in the postal organization as
Congress moves to convert the Cabinet-level department to a
quasicorporate U. S. Postal Service, with the ability to
finance itself.

ADVANCEMENT OF BUSINESS

The Department of Commerce has major responsibility
for the advancement of business, together with the Small
Business Administration.   A variety of offices and bureaus in
the Commerce Department participate in these activities, such
as--
1.   The Bureau of the Census, which conducts a decennial census of the United States, as provided in the Constitution.   This,
along with other data collection activities, provides basic statistics about the United States for use by the Government and
by private organizations or people.
2.   The Patent Office, which was established to administer
patent laws passed by Congress, as called for in the Constitution.   It also administers trademark laws.
3.   The National Bureau of Standards, which was established
in 1901, to see that science and engineering contribute to the
advancement of technology.   Its activities consist of work in
measurements and standards (basic, materials, and technological) and in technology transfer.
4.   Promotional activities, which are primarily international
activities to encourage exports.

The Small Business Administration was established in
1953 to aid and assist small business concerns.   It does this
through such activities as making loans, guaranteeing rent,
improving management skills of small business managers, and
seeing that such businesses get a "fair" portion of Government
contracts.

The other major entity under the advancement to business
subfunction is the Federal Deposit Insurance Corporation
(FDIC), which was created in 1933 to insure bank deposits and
to prevent unsound or illegal banking practices.   Because
premium receipts and interest on investments exceed claims
and expenses, the FDIC has recently shown substantial negative expenditure levels.   Activities of the Office of the Secretary

TABLE 17

Summary of Post Office Department Program,
FY's 1969-71
(In Millions of Dollars)

Item	1969a	1970b	1971b
Obligations by Major Program:			
Direct Services to Mailers	1,001	1,075	1,089
Processing of Mail	1,940	2,087	2,106
Delivery Services	2,235	2,380	2,416
Transportation	615	641	661
Enforcing Postal Laws and Regulations	28	34	37
Research, Development, and Engineering	24	48	63
Administrative Postal Support	543	630	660
Logistical Postal Support	842	1,035	1,331
Total Obligations	7,228	7,930	8,362
Financing:			
Net Postal Revenues	6,114	6,369	6,521
Additional Revenues from Proposed Rate Increase and Other Actions	---	156	1,174
Net Unobligated Budget Authority	-95	-33	84
New Budget Authority	1,209	1,438	583
Total Financing	7,228	7,930	8,362

aActual.
bEstimate.
Note: Figures may not add to totals because of rounding.

Source: The Budget, FY 1971, p. 122

in DOT are under this subfunction, as are expenditures for
the National Transportation Safety Board.

AREA AND REGIONAL DEVELOPMENT

The subfunction of area and regional development is aimed
at reducing unemployment and improving incomes in areas of
the country that are well behind other sections in terms of
economic development. This subfunction is closely tied to
the community development parts of the Housing and Community Development field and the rural development parts of
Agriculture and Rural Development. The interests, here, are
largely economic, while community development is often
thought of as including broader activities, both economic and
social. Community development is often more directly people-
oriented, whereas economic development is more often directed toward business and physical infrastructure and, indirectly through this means, provides jobs and income for
people.

Activities under this subfunction are divided among the
Appalachian Regional Development Programs, administered
by the Appalachian Regional Commission; the Economic Development Administration (EDA) of the Commerce Department;
and the Bureau of Indian Affairs in the Interior Department.
Established in 1965, the Appalachian Commission focuses exclusively on the large multistate Appalachian region. It develops plans and coordinates programs for regional economic
development, including highway system construction, health
projects, land programs, water resources survey, facility
construction, and research. The Economic Development
Administration activities cover the entire United States. Outlays are made for public-works grants and loans, industrial
or commercial facility loans, working capital loan guarantees,
and technical, planning, and research assistance. Somewhat less than half of the expenditures of the Bureau of Indian
Affairs are considered a contribution to area and regional
development, such as activities in resources management,
road construction, and tribal trust funds.

REGULATION OF BUSINESS

Included in this subfunction are a variety of activities, handled, for the most part, by a number of independent Federal regulatory agencies, which, despite their total outlays of only 1.3 percent of the Commerce function, have great influence in the field. These include the following:

1. The Commerce Department has programs to control export of strategic commodities and to regulate U. S. direct foreign investment.

2. The Justice Department Antitrust Division is responsible for enforcing the Federal antitrust and trade regulation laws, which seek to maintain competitive enterprise. The Division also represents the United States in proceedings to review decisions of many of the regulatory agencies. A Consumer Protection Division protects consumers against deceptive practices.

3. The Civil Aeronautics Board, in its regulatory activities, controls civil aviation in the United States and between the United States and foreign countries. It does this by granting authorizations to carriers for routes, authorizing rates, and regulating relations among carriers.

4. The Federal Communications Commission was created to regulate communication "by wire and radio" in interstate and foreign commerce and to provide "rapid, efficient, nationwide and worldwide . . . communication service with adequate facilities at reasonable charges . . . "[11] Its responsibilities have expanded as means of communication have expanded and now include satellite communications.

5. The Federal Maritime Commission regulates foreign and domestic offshore shipping.

6. The Federal Trade Commission is responsible for seeing that competition in trade is free and fair and, along with the Justice Department, enforces antitrust and trade regulation laws. It also shares consumer protection responsibilities with the Justice Department and regulates deceptive advertising practices.

7. The Interstate Commerce Commission regulates common carriers specified by legislation and engaged in transportation in interstate commerce.

8. The Securities and Exchange Commission administers laws designed to protect against malpractice in the securities and financial markets.

This summary of the regulatory agencies inadequately

describes their extensive power and the sometimes conflicting or outdated laws under which they operate. The regulatory
agencies have an important influence on the overall commerce,
transportation, and communications network of the United
States and have a tendency to be a force against rather than
for change. Technological developments are, oftentimes, far
in advance of the laws and practices under which these regulatory agencies, which tend to stress precedent, operate.

RESEARCH AND DEVELOPMENT

As noted earlier, R&D in the Commerce functional field
ranks about in the middle for all Government R&D expenditures by functional field. In 1971, R&D is estimated to be
4.8 percent of total outlays in the Commerce field. Table
18 shows specific R&D program areas and R&D expenditures
for 1969-71.
If the program areas are grouped by subfunction, the
breakdown is as shown in Table 19.
Because of differences in relative importance of R&D to
each subfunction, this distribution is very different from the
total expenditure distribution by subfunction in Table 15. Air
transportation, for example, which is over half of all Commerce R&D, is only a fifth of total expenditures. Ground
transportation, which is more than half of total expenditures,
is only 16 percent of R&D expenditures.

Department of Transportation (DOT)*

Federal Highway Administration and National
Highway Safety Bureau

The Federal Highway Administration conducts R&D relating mainly to traffic operations, new construction techniques,
and the social and economic aspects of highways. With respect to traffic and highway safety, the National Highway
Safety Bureau conducts comprehensive traffic safety research,
initiates training and education programs, and initiates demonstration projects to speed the implementation of new safety
techniques into practice.

---

*Descriptions of these R&D program areas are excerpted
from The Budget.

TABLE 18

Commerce, Transportation, and Communications
R&D Conduct Expenditures by Program Area, FY's 1969-71
(In Millions of Dollars)

1971 Rank	Program Area	Agency	1969a	1970b	1971b
1	Aviation Technology	NASA	161.6	173.6	176.3
2	Federal Aviation Administration	DOT	43.4	51.6	59.6
3	Federal Highway Administration	DOT	26.9	38.4	53.2
4	Post Office Department	Post Office	20.9	26.7	41.4
5	National Bureau of Standards	Commerce	27.5	29.6	30.1
6	Coast Guard	DOT	4.4	13.5	13.5
7	Other DOT R&D	DOT	5.8	10.0	13.0
8	Maritime Administration	Commerce	9.9	10.3	12.1
9	Other Commerce R&D	Commerce	9.9	12.1	9.4
10	Urban Mass Transportation Administration	DOT	1.5	5.0	7.5
11	Railroad Administration	DOT	9.1	10.5	7.4
12	Federal Communications Commission	FCC	0.8	0.8	0.7
13	Civil Aeronautics Board	CAB	0.2	0.2	0.2
14	Small Business Administration	SBA	0.2	0.1	0.1
	Total		322.1	382.4	424.5

aActual.
bEstimate.

Source: Data obtained from The Budget, FY 1971, NASA, the Department of Transportation, the Department of Commerce, and the Office of Management and Budget.

TABLE 19

Commerce, Transportation, and Communications
R&D Conduct Expenditures by Subfunction, FY 1971

Subfunction	Percent of Total
Air Transportation	55. 5
Ground Transportation	16. 0
Postal Service	9. 8
Advancement of Business, Area and Regional Development	9. 4
Water Transportation	6. 1
Other Transportation R&D	3. 1
Regulation of Business	0. 2
	100. 0

Note: Figures may not add to totals because of rounding.

Source: Data obtained from The Budget, FY 1971, NASA, the Department of Transportation, the Department of Commerce, and the Office of Management and Budget.

Federal Aviation Administration

The FAA carries out a program to improve and modernize the national system of aviation facilities through the development of new systems, procedures, and devices. The agency also carries out a program of medical research to aid in the development of rules and regulations governing the certification of airmen and to assure aviation safety.

Coast Guard

The Coast Guard conducts basic and applied scientific RDT&E on maintenance and rehabilitation, lease, and operation of facilities and equipment. Areas of investigation include aids to navigation, ships and boats, aircraft, and rescue equipment. The National Data Buoy System program initiated the developmental phase of a national system to collect oceanographic and environmental data through a worldwide system of buoys.

Federal Railroad Administration

High-speed ground transportation R&D includes materials, aerodynamics, vehicle propulsion, vehicle control, communications, guideways, and research testing on new systems, components, and techniques. Activities provide for conducting demonstrations to determine the contributions that high-speed ground transportation can make to more efficient and economical intercity transportation systems. Demonstrations of improved services are conducted to measure and evaluate public reaction and acceptance of such services. Travel needs and preferences are analyzed and performance and costs compared.

Urban Mass Transportation Administration

This agency funds R&D to assist in the development, testing, and demonstration of new ideas, methods, and technologies for improving mass transportation systems and services. Efforts are being directed toward solutions of problems in user and community acceptance, stimulating private investments in promising areas of technological innovation, and influencing institutional constraints that inhibit the development and application of new systems. Grants are provided to state and local public agencies for the planning, engineering, and designing of urban mass transportation systems.

Other DOT

Other DOT includes R&D in connection with the programs of the St. Lawrence Seaway Development Corporation and the National Transportation Safety Board.

Other Agencies

Federal Communications Commission (FCC)

The FCC regulates interstate and foreign commerce in communications by wire and radio. The FCC is required by the Communications Act to attain and maintain maximum benefits for the people of the United States in the use of the radio spectrum and regulate the rates and services of communications common carriers. The FCC conducts small amounts of research in connection with these objectives.

Federal Trade Commission (FTC)

The FTC has the duty of preserving free competitive enterprise through prevention of monopolistic and unfair trade. Its research is principally economic and statistical studies of market concentrations.

Aviation Technology (NASA)

The objective of this activity is to extend the national capability in aeronautics and to support other Government agencies having aeronautical interests and responsibilities, such as the departments of Defense and Transportation. Aviation research continues in V/STOL, subsonic, supersonic, and hypersonic technology in support of civilian and military aircraft development. Increased emphasis is being placed on research in noise reduction and alleviation.

National Bureau of Standards (NBS)

The NBS research program provides a capability and competence for many services performed by the NBS, such as publication of scientific information; calibration of measuring instruments; tests of materials, products, or systems; production and sale of standard reference materials; consultation and advice on scientific or technical problems; and specialized research on specific technical problems of other Federal agencies

Maritime Administration

Research within the Maritime Administration is directed toward joint surface effect ship programs, marine science and technology, shipping economics and requirements, advanced ship engineering and development, and improvement in ship operations and shipping systems. Primary research is in hydrodynamics, propulsion, ship structures, navigation-communications electronics, and facilities and systems to disseminate technical information.

Other Commerce

These programs include R&D efforts within the EDA (but excludes EDA's technical assistance program, which is many times larger than its research program and is principally carried out through contracts), Appalachian Assistance Program,

Business and Defense Services Administration, Office of
Business Economics, Bureau of the Census, and the Patent
Office.

Post Office

This activity includes the operations research and human
engineering programs. Operations research includes long-term
systems engineering, the application of advanced management
sciences to the R&D program, and the identification and/or
analysis and evaluation of new technological capabilities. Human engineering provides for the conduct of studies and tests
in the areas of mechanization, design, and the improvement of
environmental conditions.

NOTES

1. Executive Office of the President, Bureau of the Budget,
The Budget in Brief, FY 1968 (Washington, D.C.: U.S. Government Printing Office, 1968), p. 37.

2. U.S. Constitution Sesquicentennial Commission, His-
tory of the Formation of the Union under the Constitution, with
Liberty Documents and Report of the Commission (Washington,
D.C.: U.S. Government Printing Office, 1941), p. 12.

3. Ibid., p. 14.

4. Ibid., p. 15.

5. John F. Kennedy, Transportation Message (Washington, D.C.: The White House, April 4, 1962).

6. Ibid.

7. John P. Doyle, National Transportation Policy, 87th
Cong., 2d sess., Senate Commerce Committee Report No.
445 (Washington, D.C.: U.S. Government Printing Office, 1961).

8. The National Archives of the United States, United
States Government Organization Manual, 1968-1969 (Washington, D.C.: U.S. Government Printing Office, 1968), p. 407.

9. Ibid., p. 315.

10. Ibid., p. 231.

11. Ibid., p. 443.

CHAPTER **8** AGRICULTURE AND
RURAL DEVELOPMENT

THE FIELD AS A WHOLE

This functional field includes programs designed to support and assist the farm and rural sector of the nation's economy. The line items used here are the same as those included
under this functional field in The Budget. The individual line
items are included under the subfunctions of farm income stabilization, rural housing and public facilities, agricultural
land and water resources, and research and other agricultural
services. Programs concerned primarily with helping other
countries with their agricultural problems are included under
the International Relations functional field.

Federal agricultural policies are strongly influenced by
the nation's heritage of respect for, and dependence on, the
the land as the provider of food for the population and of employment. Despite the radical changes in agricultural production because of expanding technology, the family farm is still
looked on, publicly at least, as a backbone of the nation's
strength. This belief is rooted less in the vital contribution
that agricultural production makes to the economy than in a
somewhat nostalgic view of farming and farmers as being "close
to the earth" in a way that connotes a goodness and pureness
of life not attainable in an urban atmosphere. The stream of
farmers migrating to the cities since World War II has somewhat shaken this belief, and the growth of large, commercial
farms has left only 7 percent of the population on farms.

In his 1968 message to Congress on Agriculture, President
Johnson restated the goals set forth by Franklin D. Roosevelt
thirty years earlier, " . . . to assure agriculture a fair share
of an increasing national income, to provide consumers with
abundant supplies of food and fiber, to stop waste of soil, and
to reduce the gap between huge surpluses and disastrous short-
ages."[1] Basic to the national agricultural policies has been
the desire to provide an adequate supply of food to feed the

population--an aim that could be fairly easily related to all
three supergoals of Public Welfare, National Security, and
Economic Growth. A country with an inadequate supply of
food would obviously not be caring for the welfare of its citizens. It would be dependent on allies for food supplies and in
a precarious position regarding its enemies. It would be less
able to divert to industrial growth the capital and manpower
necessary to increase the food supply. Although many of the
less developed countries are faced quite starkly with the problem of providing an adequate supply of food for their people,
the situation in the United States has been just the opposite--
one of overabundance. The second goal of Franklin D. Roosevelt
has been met to overflowing.

    It is the first goal that has caused a great deal of trouble--
that of assuring agriculture a "fair share" of an increasing
national income. The policy designed to accomplish this has
been the concept of "parity," given legal status in the Agricultural Adjustment Act of 1938. This became the basis of
price supports and was designed to provide farmers with a
"fair" return for their products, based on receipts that, in
the past, had been deemed fair. If what a farmer purchases
has gone up in price a certain percentage since the established
base period, he would be at 100 percent of parity if the products
he sells have also gone up by that percent. Otherwise, the
Government would subsidize him for at least part of the difference under various price support programs. The methods
devised to carry out these policies are discussed in more detail in the individual sections that follow.

    Before discussing the specific agricultural programs, the
following figures will show where Agriculture and Rural Development stands vis-à-vis other functional fields of Government activity. As Table 2 in Chapter 2 shows, the dollar
amounts allocated to this field and the percent of total of all
outlays over the 1961 to 1971 period have varied considerably
in response to crop yields. Starting with 1961, when outlays
were $3.3 billion, they rose to $5.2 billion in 1964, were back
down to $3.7 billion in 1966, up again to an estimated $6.3
billion in 1970, and down to an estimated $5.4 billion in 1971.
These outlays reflected percentages of the total budget ranging
from a low of 2.9 percent in 1966, 1967, and 1971 to a high of
4.9 percent in 1963. Over the eleven-year period, the percent
of total has decreased by 0.7 percent. The ranking of Agriculture and Rural Development outlays has remained approximately in the middle of all functional fields, moving from fifth
to sixth place over the 1961-71 period, as shown in Table 4 in
Chapter 2.

In R&D conduct expenditures, Agriculture and Rural Development was also ranked just about in the middle in both 1961 and 1971. Its R&D expenditures amounted to 1.4 percent of all Government R&D expenditures in 1961 and 1.7 percent in 1971. As a percent of total outlays, R&D was 3.6 percent in 1961 and 4.8 percent in 1971; once again, it ranked about in the middle, with some fields having a much higher R&D content and others much lower.

Overall outlays for Agriculture and Rural Development appear in Table 20, which shows the details of actual 1969 and estimated 1970 and 1971 outlays. These outlays are almost exclusively the responsibility of the Department of Agriculture.

FARM INCOME STABILIZATION

This subfunction accounts for over 70 percent of Agriculture and Rural Development outlays and is the area on which most division can be found as to its appropriateness as an instrument of policy.

Price Support and Related Programs

The concept of parity, mentioned before, is the backbone of the policy of farm income stabilization. The Agricultural Adjustment Act of 1938 is the basic law that set forth price supports and related quotas and acreage allotments. The Commodity Credit Corporation (CCC), through the Agricultural Stabilization and Conservation Service, handles the price support and production stabilization programs. Policies have varied for different commodities, including some commodities with no production controls and some with minimum acreage allotments, which were well above the amount the market could absorb, thus still creating large surpluses. Also, acreage controls do not necessarily control production as marginal land is eliminated and as farmers use better fertilizer. When crop yields are such as to depress the market price below what the Government has set as that year's price support, surplus commodities are purchased at the price support level by the Government, thus elevating the market price near the agreed upon level. When acreage allotments still produce excessive supplies, marketing quotas may also be used if two-thirds of the producers agree on such quotas.

TABLE 20

Agriculture and Rural Development Outlay Details, FY's 1969-71
(In Millions of Dollars)

Program or Agency	Outlays		
	1969[a]	1970[b]	1971[b]
Farm Income Stabilization (Department of Agriculture):			
Price Support and Related Programs	4, 114	3, 541	3, 704
Long-Term Land Retirement Programs	189	120	80
Removal of Surplus Agricultural Commodities	415	471	462
National Wool Act	68	58	65
Sugar Act	87	93	88
Agricultural and Emergency Credit Programs (Less Net			
Asset Sales)[c]	-47	-16	-114
Other[c]	174	217	181
Total, Farm Income Stabilization	5, 000	4, 485	4, 467
Rural Housing and Public Facilities (Agriculture):			
Rural Electrification and Telephones	314	369	339
Rural Housing (Less Net Asset Sales)	13	341	-627
Rural Water and Waste Disposal Grants	28	34	31
Other[c]	-37	86	81
Agricultural Land and Water Resources (Agriculture):			
Soil Conservation Service--Conservation Operations	117	127	130
Agricultural Conservation Program Payments			
(Including Commodity Credit Corporation Loans)	194	183	152
Other[c]	32	34	35
Research and Other Agricultural Services (Agriculture):			
Research and Extension Programs[c]	437	482	542
Consumer Protective, Marketing, and Regulatory Programs[c]	152	184	191
Other[c]	56	61	66
Deductions for Offsetting Receipts:			
Interfund and Intragovernmental Transactions	-6	-3	---
Proprietary Receipts from the Public	-79	-39	-41
Total	6, 221	6, 343	5, 364

[a]Actual.
[b]Estimate.
[c]Includes both Federal funds and trust funds.
Note: Figures may not add to totals because of rounding.

Source: Edited excerpts from The Budget, FY 1971, p. 102.

Long-Term Land Retirement Programs

Three programs under this line item are designed to reduce excess production by changing land-use patterns away
from agriculture. Under the Conservation Reserve Program
(the Soil Bank Act of 1956), farmers retired cropland for conservation uses for a stipulated period of time. Contract authority for this program ended in 1960, and all contracts are
scheduled to expire by 1972. Under the Cropland Conversion
Program (under the Food and Agriculture Act of 1962), cropland better suited to other purposes was to be permanently
changed and croplands not presently needed were to be tem-
porarily changed. Under the Cropland Adjustment Program
(Food and Agriculture Act of 1965), cropland was to be con-
verted to develop and conserve various other resources, such
as water and wildlife.

Removal of Surplus Agricultural Commodities

The Consumer and Marketing Service of the Agriculture
Department is responsible for outlays under this line item,
and it attempts to expand the demand for products through payments to exporters and payments to divert surplus commodities
to new uses and markets. Surplus commodities are also distributed to school lunch programs and to welfare programs.

National Wool Act

The National Wool Act of 1954 has resulted, generally,
in wool producers selling their product on the open market for
whatever they could get and then receiving a direct payment
from the Government for the difference between this price and
a higher support price, thus benefiting both producer and user.
This was designed to encourage domestic production of wool.

Sugar Act

Quotas have been a custom--both domestic and foreign--
to assure United States producers of a substantial portion of
the U.S. sugar market, despite lower-priced competition from
abroad. Payments are also made to domestic producers.

Agriculture and Emergency Credit Programs

The activities of the Farm Credit Administration (not a part of the Department of Agriculture) come under this line item. They consist, primarily, of providing credit to farmers for cooperative activities, such as marketing and purchasing.

Other

This line item consists of salaries for personnel in the Agricultural Stabilization and Conservation Service and a small amount for administrative and operating expenses of the Federal Crop Insurance Corporation, which insures against unavoidable losses.

The above line items, all falling under the subfunction "Farm Income Stabilization," make up over 70 percent of all Agriculture and Rural Development outlays, and, in a sense, contribute to the Welfare and Income Security function, since they were designed as income-sustaining programs for those whose incomes would otherwise not provide an adequate standard of living. In actual practice, much of the subsidy does not go to the family farmer but to larger commercial farmers.

RURAL HOUSING AND PUBLIC FACILITIES

This subfunction includes a significant amount of lending and repayment of Government loans, as well as the sale of such loans to financial institutions. As a result, outlay figures vary considerably and are negative when repayments or loan sales exceed new loans, as is expected in FY 1971. The subfunction accounted for 5 percent of the Agriculture and Rural Development outlays in FY 1969 and 13 percent in FY 1970.

Rural Electrification and Telephones

The Rural Electrification Administration, established in 1936 under the Rural Electrification Act, makes loans for rural electrification and telephone service on an area basis. A private bank is being established to provide additional financing for rural electrification borrowers. Consideration is being given to creating a telephone bank of mixed-- and, eventually, private--ownership to provide credit for rural telephone systems at commercially competitive rates.

Rural Housing, Water, and Waste Disposal

It is estimated that about half of the substandard housing in the United States is in rural areas. Financial and technical assistance to low- and moderate-income rural residents is provided for building, buying, or renting adequate housing or for repairing existing housing. The Farmers Home Administration administers programs to provide rural housing and, also, administers programs to provide water and sewer loans for rural water and waste disposal facilities.

AGRICULTURAL LAND AND WATER RESOURCES

Activities under this subfunction are aimed, primarily, at conservation of land and water as a long-term policy for the resources involved rather than, primarily, as a means of affecting the market price of crops that otherwise would have been grown on the lands. The two major conservation programs are those of the Soil Conservation Service and the Agricultural Stabilization and Conservation Service, which also handles the price support program.

The Soil Conservation Service, established in 1935, carries out a program of soil and water conservation, involving erosion control and sediment reduction, flood prevention, land-use planning in rural areas, recreation, and water development. Technical help is given to local soil conservation districts, and soil surveys are conducted as a basis for planning. Activities concerned primarily with watershed planning and flood control are included under Natural Resources.

The conservation activities of the Agricultural Stabilization and Conservation Service have been in existence since 1936 and involve a program of cost-sharing whereby the Government assumes part of the cost of soil and water conservation practices, which would not otherwise be done by the owners involved. Conservation practices include providing and protecting vegetative cover for lands, protection from wind and water erosion, wildlife protection, and water conservation. Disaster conservation measures are also supported. The Budget proposes to terminate the agricultural conservation cost-sharing program to help provide resources for higher priority programs.

RESEARCH AND OTHER AGRICULTURAL SERVICES

This subfunction accounts for 10 percent to 15 percent of
Agriculture and Rural Development outlays. The other agricultural services include: Farmer Cooperative Service, Statistical Reporting Service, Consumer and Marketing Service,
Rural Community Development Service, Office of Inspector
General, Packers and Stockyards Administration, Office of
the General Counsel, Office of Information, National Agricultural Library, Office of Management Services, and General
Administration. The objectives of these programs are, generally, to provide information, technical assistance, and various other services in order to help both producers and consumer
as well as provide general management and administrative functions in the Department of Agriculture. R&D programs and
expenditures are described below.

RESEARCH AND DEVELOPMENT

As noted earlier, R&D in Agriculture and Rural Development ranks about in the middle in importance of R&D to the
Government, as compared with other fields, with 1.7 percent
of total R&D expenditures in 1971. R&D has grown 116 percent
since 1961 (or $139 million), which is low compared with the
growth of R&D in the other fields, except National Security.
R&D has grown slightly in its percent of all Agriculture and
Rural Development outlays, but is still only 4.8 percent of
these outlays in 1971, as contrasted with 3.6 percent in 1961.
As Table 21 shows, the Agricultural Research Service accounts
for over 60 percent of the R&D conduct expenditures in the
Agriculture and Rural Development field. The Cooperative
State Research Service is second most important, accounting
for 25 percent to 28 percent, and the Economic Research Service is third most important, accounting for only 6 percent.
These three programs, together, account for over 95 percent
of all Agriculture and Rural Development R&D conduct expenditures.

TABLE 21

Agriculture and Rural Development R&D Conduct
Expenditures by Program Area, FY's 1969-71
(In Millions of Dollars)

Program Area	1969[a]	1970[b]	1971[b]
Agricultural Research Service	156.4	156.3	160.9
Cooperative State Research Service	57.9	61.0	71.6
Economic Research Service	13.0	14.5	16.4
Fertilizer R&D			
(Tennessee Valley Authority)	4.4	4.6	4.8
Special Agricultural Investigations			
(Tennessee Valley Authority)	0.2	0.2	0.3
Other	3.8	4.2	4.7
Total	235.7	240.8	258.7

[a]Actual.
[b]Estimate.

Source: Data obtained from the Department of Agriculture
and the Tennessee Valley Authority.

Department of Agriculture*

Agricultural Research Service

This service conducts basic and applied research relating
to the production, utilization, and marketing of agricultural
products, research on nutrition and consumer use, and it carries out those control and regulatory programs of the Department that involve enforcement of plant and animal quarantine,
the control of diseases and pests of animals and plants, and
related work.

Cooperative State Research Service

This service administers funds for payments and grants
to state agricultural experiment stations and other eligible

---

*Descriptions of these R&D program areas are excerpted
from The Budget.

institutions for the support of research in agriculture, the
rural home, the rural community, and forestry. This service
involves supervision of the funds and close advisory relations
with the state agricultural experiment stations, schools of
forestry, and other institutions eligible to receive funds. It
participates in planning and coordination of research programs
among the states and between the states and the Department of
Agriculture.

Economic Research Service

This service conducts research to measure, appraise,
and analyze on a continuing basis, economic changes that occur
in farming and in the use of human and natural rural resources
and to indicate needed adjustments.

Other Agriculture

Other agriculture research activities not listed above in-
clude small programs of the National Agricultural Library,
Farmer Cooperative Service, Statistical Reporting Service,
Soil Conservation Service, and Consumer and Marketing Service.

Tennessee Valley Authority

The Tennessee Valley Authority (TVA) conducts scientific
R&D activities under its responsibilities to aid in the unified
development of the resources of the region, to develop and
test new or improved chemical fertilizers, and to improve the
efficiency of its operations.

Agronomic research is undertaken to evaluate new TVA
fertilizer materials, by greenhouse and field plot tests, as to
availability of plant food to plants, reactions with the soil, and
use practices. Small-scale chemical laboratory research and
pilot-plant experimentation are conducted in the development
of new or improved fertilizer products and processes, and
technological studies of plant operations are conducted. Economic analyses of the Tennessee Valley agriculture are made
for program planning and evaluation purposes and the examination of special regional farm problems.

NOTES

1. Franklin D. Roosevelt, 1938, as quoted in Lyndon B. Johnson's Message on Agriculture, February 27, 1968 (Washington, D.C.: The White House, 1968).

CHAPTER **9** GENERAL GOVERNMENT

THE FIELD AS A WHOLE

The functional field entitled "General Government," as described in The Budget, includes programs providing for "Government-wide service activities, for executive direction and financial management, for programs of law enforcement and criminal justice, and for the costs of the Congress and the Federal Court system."[1] No changes have been made in the field for this study.

Without the elements of Government included in this functional field, the work of other functional fields would, eventually, grind to a halt; laws would not be passed, the budget would not be prepared and monitored, taxes would not be collected, and the President would be without a staff and, in fact, without a salary himself. Government activities in this functional field provide the basic structure or framework for initiating, interpreting, and carrying out the "will of the people." The three traditional arms of the Government are found here-- Executive, Legislative, and Judicial. Although this field contains many of the more mundane aspects of Government (such as printing the Congressional Record each night and delivering copies to the Congressmen each morning), it also contains some of the more controversial aspects of the Government (such as law enforcement and civil rights activities, the Supreme Court, and hearings by Congressional Committees).

The General Government functional field is essentially synonymous with the fourth supergoal discussed in Chapter 1, also entitled "General Government." Although, in a sense, the general operations of the Government ultimately contribute to the other supergoals (National Security, Public Welfare, Economic Development), the goal of maintaining a functioning government is basic enough to stand alone. Because this country has been able to achieve a functioning government with relative ease (the Civil War being the major exception), it is easy to forget how vital government is in order to achieve other

116

major goals. Increasing societal tensions during the past few years have reawakened concern for the attainment and maintenance of this goal and brought the realization that no country is immune to the kinds of internal disorders that can disrupt a society and its government.

The proportion of Federal funds devoted to this field in 1971 is 2.2 percent, compared with 1.6 percent in 1961. Outlays showed a slow but steady rise from $1.5 billion in 1961 to $2.9 billion in 1969. In the last few years, this amount has risen to $4 billion, making the field seventh in rank in 1971 compared to ninth (out of twelve) in 1961.

R&D expenditures are small ($1 million in 1961, $17 million in 1971), smaller than any other field. R&D in this field was only 0.1 percent of total Government R&D expenditures in 1971, and was only 0.4 percent of total General Government functional field outlays.

A more detailed look at overall outlays for General Government appears in Table 22, which shows the actual 1969, and estimated 1970 and 1971, outlays, as given in The Budget, broken down by subfunctions and areas under these subfunctions.

A wide variety of Government bodies (many very small and, often, temporary) account for outlays in this field. Total outlays for 1971, by agency or body, are indicated in Table 23.

The following briefly summarizes the responsibilities under the subfunctions of the General Government field as shown in Table 22.

LEGISLATIVE FUNCTIONS

Outlays for legislative functions cover essentially all expenses associated with the Congress, expenses such as salaries of the members of Congress and their staffs, expenses for investigations and other committee work, building construction and upkeep, and printing and binding done by the Government Printing Office. A few aspects of the Legislative branch that are not included in this subfunction are the Library of Congress (included in the Education, Knowledge, and Manpower field) and expenses of the General Accounting Office (included below under the subfunction "Central Fiscal Operations").

TABLE 22

General Government Outlay Details, FY's 1969-71
(In Millions of Dollars)

Program or Agency	Outlays		
	1969[a]	1970[b]	1971[b]
Legislative Functions	192	234	242
Judicial Functions	110	130	135
Executive Direction and Management	31	41	45
Central Fiscal Operations:			
Treasury Department:			
Internal Revenue Service	746	848	904
Other[c]	283	333	360
Other Agencies[c]	65	76	82
General Property and Records Management:			
General Services Administration:			
Construction, sites, and planning	88	90	98
Operation, maintenance, and other[c]	480	542	533
Other agencies[c]	d	d	2
Central Personnel Management:			
Civil Service Commission:[e]			
Present program	79	85	96
Proposed legislation	---	---	3
Department of Labor and other[c]	68	81	85
Law Enforcement and Justice:			
Department of Justice[c]	508	735	975
Other Agencies	26	37	53
National Capital Region:			
District of Columbia:			
Present program	154	228	227
Proposed legislation	---	7	63
Rapid Transit	6	20	122
Other	1	2	2
Other General Government:			
Territories and Possessions	209	228	238
Treasury Claims	62	156	66
Other	-3	1	10
Deductions for Offsetting Receipts:			
Interfund and Intragovernmental Transactions[e]	-92	-103	-108
Proprietary Receipts from the Public	-146	-150	-147
Total	2,866	3,620	4,084

[a]Actual.

[b]Estimate.

[c]Includes both Federal funds and trust funds.

[d]Less than $0.5 million.

[e]Excludes payments to trust fund to arrest increase in unfunded liability to the retirement program (1969, $71 million; 1970, $73 million; 1971, $236 million).

Note: Figures may not add to totals because of rounding.

Source: Edited excerpts from The Budget, FY 1971, p. 183.

TABLE 23

General Government Outlays by Agency, FY 1971
(In Millions of Dollars)

Agency	Dollars	Percent of Total
Treasury Department	1,466	33.8
Justice Department	975	22.5
General Services Administration	631	14.5
Legislative Branch	324	7.5
District of Columbia	290	6.7
Federal Judiciary	134	3.1
Washington Metropolitan Area Transit Authority	122	2.8
Civil Service Commission	99	2.3
Department of the Interior	87	2.0
Department of Labor	85	2.0
Department of Defense	60	1.4
Executive Office of the President	42	1.0
Other	23	0.5
Subtotal	4,339	100.0
Adjustments	- 255	
Total Outlays	4,084	

Note: Figures may not add to totals because of rounding.

Source: Data compiled from The Budget, FY 1971, Table 14, pp. 571-83.

JUDICIAL FUNCTIONS

Outlays of the Federal Judiciary comprise this subfunction--that is, outlays by the Supreme Court, primarily for salaries, and outlays for other Federal Courts and judicial services, such as Courts of Appeals, District Courts, and referees.

EXECUTIVE DIRECTION AND MANAGEMENT

Smallest in outlays of all the General Government sub-functions, this category provides for the executive operations that are closest to the President and are generally called his "Executive Office." The salaries of the President and his White House staff are included here. A number of groups that provide executive advice and/or management are included also, such as the following:

1.   Office of Management and Budget, which prepares and re-views the annual budget, supervises its administration once passed, tries to improve Government management, and serves in other important capacities as a general source of advice and supervision for the President

2.   Council of Economic Advisors, established by the Employ-ment Act of 1946 to advise the President on the state of the economy and on economic programs and policies of the Federal Government

3.   National Security Council, established in 1947 to advise the President on all national policies that relate to national security

4.   Domestic Council, established in 1970 to advise the Presi-dent on all domestic national policies

5.   National Aeronautics and Space Council, established in 1958 to "advise and assist the President regarding policies, plans, and programs; to fix the responsibilities of the United States agencies engaged in aeronautical and space activities and to develop a comprehensive program of such activities"[2]

6.   Office of Emergency Preparedness, which sets and co-ordinates policies relating to emergency preparedness activities, such as civil defense; determination of necessary strategic materials; plans for resource use in emergencies; and plans for Government organization in emergencies

7.   Office of Science and Technology, established in 1962 to advise the President on policies and programs in science and technology.

CENTRAL FISCAL OPERATIONS

Most outlays for this subfunction are handled by the Treasury Department, and central fiscal operations account for most Treasury Department outlays other than interest on the national debt (which is not included in this functional field analysis). The Treasury Department was created in 1789 to manage the nation's finances. Some of the bureaus responsible for this subfunction are the Bureau of Accounts, the Bureau of Customs, Bureau of the Mint, Bureau of Public Debt, and the Internal Revenue Service. Outlays by the Internal Revenue Service for collecting and processing taxes make up the bulk of outlays. Its outlays alone are greater than the total outlays for any other General Government subfunction. Outlays by groups other than the Treasury Department are mainly for the General Accounting Office.

GENERAL PROPERTY AND RECORDS MANAGEMENT

The General Services Administration accounts for outlays under this heading. It is responsible for managing the property and records of the Government, including such aspects as construction and operation of buildings, keeping of records, and procurement and distribution of supplies.

CENTRAL PERSONNEL MANAGEMENT

Outlays by the Civil Service Commission for its own operation make up most of this subfunction, with some outlays by the Bureau of Employees' Compensation of the Labor Department. This latter Bureau provides compensation for Federal workers who are injured on the job. The Civil Service Commission is responsible for hiring most Federal employees under a merit system.

LAW ENFORCEMENT AND JUSTICE

Law enforcement and justice has been of great concern in the last few years and is likely to be more so for the near future. Most activities of the Justice Department are covered by this subfunction and include The Budget headings of Legal Activities and General Administration, Federal Bureau of Investigation, Immigration and Naturalization Service, Federal Prison System, Bureau of Narcotics and Dangerous Drugs, and Law Enforcement Assistance Administration.

The 1968 Safe Streets and Crime Control Act provided for a variety of grants to states--for planning, law enforcement assistance, and for training and research. These grants are administered by the Law Enforcement Assistance Administration (LEAA). Also established within the Justice Department was a National Institute of Law Enforcement and Criminal Justice to fund research and demonstrations in law enforcement methods. Although the Federal Government is still unlikely to participate directly in local law enforcement, it is clear that Federal money can be used indirectly to affect law enforcement on the local level.

In addition to having responsibilities for crime control, the Justice Department has major responsibilities for enforcement of the various Civil Rights bills that were passed in the 1960's.

NATIONAL CAPITAL REGION

Because of the special relationship between the Federal Government and the District of Columbia, the Government has had primary responsibility and control over the local District of Columbia government, though home rule has been an issue for many years. At present, District of Columbia funds come largely from local taxes, a Federal contribution (in lieu of taxes on Federal property), and Federal loans, but Congress must approve the District of Columbia budget before any money can be spent. The outlays listed under this subfunction are the Federal payment (under expenditures) and the Federal loans (under net lending). Most of the increase of funding is for the Metropolitan Rapid Transit System, to be constructed during the 1970's.

OTHER GENERAL GOVERNMENT

Outlays for this subfunction are, primarily, for payments to various geographical entities under the jurisdiction of the

United States: Puerto Rico, Virgin Islands, Panama Canal, and various Pacific territories, such as Guam and the Trust Territory of the Pacific. Outlays are made by the departments of Defense, Interior, and Treasury.

This completes discussion of the subfunctions under General Government and shows the wide range of activities included in this function. Total estimated 1971 outlays by subfunction are summarized in Table 24.

RESEARCH AND DEVELOPMENT

As noted earlier, R&D expenditures in this field are a very small part of all R&D expenditures or of all outlays in this General Government function. R&D expenditures for 1969-71 are shown in Table 25.

Department of Justice (LEAA)*

The R&D arm of LEAA is the National Institute of Law Enforcement and Criminal Justice. It is the purpose of the Institute to encourage R&D to improve and strengthen law enforcement by conducting and funding research in relevant sciences. Authority also exists for research fellowships, special workshops, formulation of recommendations for action, collection and dissemination of information, and the establishment of a research center.

Department of the Treasury
(Bureau of Engraving and Printing)

This Bureau designs, manufactures, and supplies almost all major evidences of a financial character (e.g., coins, bills, medals) issued by the United States. It designs, develops, and drafts specifications for machinery and equipment; develops electronic methods for production activities; conducts chemical, metallurgical, and engineering studies; plans and conducts continuous laboratory research, both experimental and developmental, in the fields of chemistry and physics, including studies

---

*Research program area descriptions are excerpted from The Budget or from material received from the agency.

TABLE 24

General Government Outlays by Subfunction, FY 1971
(In Millions of Dollars)

Subfunction	Dollars	Percent of Total
Central Fiscal Operations	1,345	31.0
Law Enforcement and Justice	1,027	23.7
General Property and Records Management	632	14.6
National Capital Region	414	9.5
Legislative Functions	242	5.6
Central Personnel Management	184	4.2
Judicial Functions	135	3.1
Executive Direction and Management	45	1.0
Other General Government	315	7.3
Subtotal	4,339	100.0
Adjustments	- 255	
Total Outlays	4,084	

Source: The Budget, FY 1971, p. 183.

TABLE 25

General Government R&D Conduct Expenditures
by Program Area, FY's 1969-71
(In Millions of Dollars)

Program Area	1969[a]	1970[b]	1971[b]
Department of Justice (Law Enforcement Administration)	5.4	8.4	16.6
Treasury Department	0.6	0.6	0.7
Total	6.0	9.0	17.3

[a]Actual.
[b]Estimate.

Source: Data obtained from the Office of Management and Budget.

in spectrography, spectrophotometry, microscopy, photomicrography, photography, and rheology incident to the improvement of equipment and materials.

NOTES

1.   Executive Office of the President, Bureau of the Budget, The Budget in Brief, FY 1969 (Washington, D. C.: U. S. Government Printing Office, 1968).

2.   The National Archives of the United States, United States Government Organization Manual, 1968-1969 (Washington, D. C.: U. S. Government Printing Office, 1968), p. 60.

CHAPTER **10** INTERNATIONAL RELATIONS

THE FIELD AS A WHOLE

The functional field of International Relations includes programs through which the United States seeks "to advance its essential interests and to participate as a force for peace and progress in international affairs."[1] As presented in The Budget, the functional field includes the following subfunctions: economic and financial assistance, Food for Peace, foreign information and exchange activities, and conduct of foreign affairs. No changes have been made for this study.

Responsibility for handling the conduct of foreign affairs is one of the functions that defines an independent state and, as such, has always been a permanent responsibility of the U.S. Government. This may be considered in a fairly restricted sense, as was George Washington's desire in his dictum against entangling alliances. Or, it may be looked on more broadly, as the United States has done since World War II, to include a multitude of economic, political, and military relationships, such as alliances and aid programs.

Of the supergoals noted in Chapter 1, the functional field of International Relations is directly and almost exclusively related to the goal of National Security and International Relations. Its connection with the goal of Economic Development in the United States can be made with the proposition that the nation's economic health is, in many ways, closely related to the economic health of other countries in the total world economy Foreign countries provide both raw materials for U.S. industrial production (and many manufactured goods as well) and markets for U.S. products. The relations of the United States with other countries strongly influence this country's trade patterns. But the importance of this functional field to the supergoal of Economic Growth is small in comparison with its fundamental contribution to the supergoal of National Security and International Relations.

126

The amount of attention paid to aspects of this field in Presidential messages is far greater than its relative outlays would indicate. Whereas, in many fields, there may be one message, it is not unusual for many messages in a year to deal with matters that fall within the International Relations field. In 1967, for example, there were messages on Foreign Aid, Food for India, the Asian Development Bank, and the Latin American Summit Meeting.[2] Other messages in the last few years have dealt with such topics as world health and education, United Nations charter revision, and immigration. Many of these issues are not "expenditure" oriented--it costs little to modify immigration laws. Other issues are almost limitless in terms of potential expenditures (e.g., world health, education, and foreign aid) but are not a constitutional responsibility of the Government and continue only at the sufferance of an increasingly restive Congress and, ultimately, the United States public.

The allocation of Government funds to the functional field of International Relations has ranged from a high of 4.4 percent of total outlays in 1962 to a low of 1.9 percent in 1971, as shown in Table 2. There was a drop in percent of total over the 1961-71 period, and dollar outlays are only slightly higher now than in 1961. International Relations ranked eighth (out of twelve) fields in 1971 and fourth in 1961--a large drop in relative priority.

From the standpoint of R&D, the field ranked eleventh in 1971 (with R&D expenditures of $28 million), down from tenth in 1961 (with $5 million). R&D as a percent of the International Relations field is only 0.8 percent in 1971 and is 0.2 percent of total R&D in 1971. The minor importance of R&D in this field's outlays should not obscure a related fact--that technical assistance, which, in essence, conveys to others the results of our R&D and technical expertise in other fields, is an important element of our foreign aid program.

A more detailed view of overall outlays for International Relations appears in Table 26, which shows the actual 1969, and estimated 1970 and 1971, outlays, as given in The Budget, broken down according to subfunctions and areas within these subfunctions.

The outlays shown in Table 26 are distributed among a number of agencies, with the Department of State, including the Agency for International Development (AID), and the Department of Agriculture responsible for most of the funds. This breakdown is shown in Table 27.

TABLE 26

International Relations Outlay Details, FY's 1969-71
(In Millions of Dollars)

Program or Agency	Outlays		
	1969[a]	1970[b]	1971[b]
Economic and Financial Assistance:			
Agency for International Development (AID):			
Development loans	540	458	427
Technical cooperation[c]	198	178	181
Alliance for Progress	374	371	366
Supporting assistance	474	461·	513
Contingencies and other	346	293	235
Subtotal, Agency for International Development[c]	1,931	1,761	1,720
International Financial Institutions:			
Present programs	121	250	285
Proposed legislation	- - -	6	50
Export-Import Bank	246	600	195
Peace Corps[c]	105	102	100
Overseas Private Investment Corporation	- - -	- - -	-16
Other:[c]			
Present program	18	25	20
Proposed legislation	- - -	- - -	4
Food for Peace (Agriculture)	975	971	852
Foreign Information and Exchange Activities:			
United States Information Agency[c]	184	197	195
Department of State and Other[c]	53	40	45
Conduct of Foreign Affairs:			
Department of State[c]	357	381	398
U.S. Arms Control and Disarmament Agency	10	11	10
Tariff Commission	4	4	4
Foreign Claims Settlement Commission	1	1	1
Deductions for Offsetting Receipts:			
Interfund and Intragovernmental Transactions	d	d	d
Proprietary Receipts from the Public	-217	-236	-273
Total	3,785	4,113	3,589

[a]Actual.
[b]Estimate.
[c]Includes both Federal funds and trust funds.
[d]Less than $0.5 million.
Note: Figures may not add to totals because of rounding.

Source: Edited excerpts from The Budget, FY 1971, p. 91.

TABLE 27

International Relations Outlays by Agency, FY 1971
(In Millions of Dollars)

Agency	Dollars	Percent of Total
Department of State (including AID)	2, 156[a]	55.8
Department of Agriculture	852	22.1
International Financial Institutions	335[a]	8.7
Export-Import Bank	195	5.0
United States Information Agency	195	5.0
Peace Corps	100[a]	2.6
Other	30	0.8
	3, 862	100.0
Proprietary Receipts from Public	-273	
Total Outlays	3, 589	

[a]Mostly appropriated to the President.
Note: Figures may not add to totals because of rounding.

Source: Data compiled from The Budget, FY 1971, Table 14, pp. 571-83.

The following sections treat the elements that make up the International Relations functional field in greater depth in terms of goals, objectives, policies, and programs.

ECONOMIC AND FINANCIAL ASSISTANCE

Agency for International Development

The bulk of expenditures under this subfunction is for programs carried out by the Agency for International Development (AID) with funds appropriated to the President. Foreign economic aid (military assistance is under the National Security field) achieved major backing as an instrument of foreign policy after World War II, with the Truman Doctrine of aid to Greece and Turkey and the Marshall Plan aid for European economic recovery. Under Truman's Point IV program, enunciated in 1949, the fourth point was:

> Fourth, we must embark on a bold new program for
> making the benefits of our scientific advances and
> industrial progress available for the improvement
> and growth of underdeveloped areas . . . I believe
> that we should make available to peace-loving peoples
> the benefits of our store of technical knowledge in
> order to help them realize their aspirations for a
> better life. And, in cooperation with other nations,
> we should foster capital investment in areas needing
> development. [3]

The rationale and objectives of foreign aid programs have
been multiple and, perhaps, even difficult to ascertain. There
have really been a multiplicity of objectives, and questions are
frequently raised as to the efficacy of foreign aid in achieving
some of these objectives. The basic objective of the Marshall
Plan was to bring about European economic recovery and,
thereby, avert Communist take-overs, stemming from dis-
satisfaction of the populations. This program has generally
been regarded as a very successful one.
      Later, economic aid programs began to focus on the under-
developed countries, with the principal rationale being that as
countries developed economically and socially, and as their
populations achieved higher per capita incomes, they would
be more stable, more concerned with individual aspirations
and, therefore, more democratic, and more peaceful and
responsible in the world community. It was thought that the
country providing aid would, in addition to achieving indirect
benefits from these outcomes, achieve other more direct benefits, such as maintaining a friendly government, receiving
popular gratitude, and receiving support in world public opinion.
It was also hoped that the United States might be able to influence the recipient government in some of its policies and,
perhaps, receive political advantages or favors in exchange
for aid. Finally, foreign aid has been justified as a morally
necessary act by a very wealthy country in support of less-
favored or underdeveloped countries. The multiplicity of our
goals in foreign aid; their possible conflicting nature; the difficulty of measuring their achievement; and our own internal
and external problems have put foreign aid development programs in a rather beleaguered position. Although all Presidents since World War II have supported foreign aid programs
as being in the national interest, Congress, at times, has
questioned this assumption.
      Late in the 1960's, Congress requested that the President

make a thorough review of the foreign aid program. A Task
Force on International Development was established in 1969,
headed by Rudolph A. Peterson, President of the Bank of
America. The report, submitted in 1970, recommended substantial changes in the aid program.[4] International lending
institutions, it suggested, should be the major channel for development assistance, rather than channeling most funds bi-
laterally. Economic and military aid should be funded separately.
It recommended the establishment of two independent agencies
to replace AID--one a U.S. International Development Bank
to administer bilateral development loans and the other a U.S.
International Development Institute to administer technical assistance programs. A council would be set up to coordinate
all aid activities and policies. Although not setting a specific
standard for how high a funding level should be authorized, the
Task Force did say that the recent downward trend should be
reversed and aid should not be tied to one-year appropriations
by Congress.

Table 26 shows the various line item expenditures that
make up the AID program. The types of AID expenditures are
as follows:
1. Development loans are made to assist in development
through long-range plans in less-developed friendly countries.
They are repayable in dollars.
2. Technical cooperation programs are aimed, largely, at
creating human and institutional resources necessary for development and are, generally, provided on a grant basis.
3. The Alliance for Progress was established to promote economic and social development in Latin America by assisting
in long-range plans that incorporate certain features thought
necessary for economic or social reform and development, by
self-help contributions, and by regional cooperation.
4. Supporting Assistance, a short-term form of aid, is provided to help maintain political and economic stability in countries that are contributing to various security programs in
which we have an interest.
5. Contingencies and Other largely covers situations that require action not foreseen at the time the budget was developed.

Other Economic and Financial Programs

The above AID programs account for over two-thirds of
all expenditures under the subfunction "Economic and Financial
Assistance." Other expenditures are for the following programs:

1. International financial institutions promote economic development and are funded and administered on a multinational
basis. They include the Inter-American Development Bank,
the Asian Development Bank, and the International Development
Association (associated with the World Bank).
2. The Export-Import Bank is designed to promote the growth
of United States exports through loan, insurance, and guarantee
programs. Outlays include guarantees and insurance to protect exports from commercial or political risk. Loans are
made to finance the sale of U.S. exports.
3. The Peace Corps was established to promote world peace
and friendship by providing volunteer service to other countries
to help in the manpower needs for economic and social development and to promote better understanding between peoples.

FOOD FOR PEACE

The Food for Peace program consolidated both agricultural
and foreign policy aims with passage of the Agricultural Trade
Development and Assistance Act of 1954 (Public Law 480). It
combined a desire to reduce the food surpluses produced in
the United States with a desire to satisfy some of the needs of
many less developed countries who did not produce adequate
supplies of food for their own populations. The basic means
of doing this was by selling products to foreign countries pay-
able in their own currencies and then spending these currencies
largely in the foreign countries, either for such U.S. expenses
as military bases or for economic development aid. Other
aspects of Public Law 480 involve donations rather than sales.
Emphasis has been placed recently on combining Public Law
480 and development aid--so that both may be most effective--
and on self-help commitments by recipient countries. The
percentage of payments being made in dollars or in currencies
convertible to dollars has been increasing.

FOREIGN INFORMATION AND EXCHANGE ACTIVITIES

This subfunction includes expenditures by the United States
Information Agency (USIA) and education exchange programs
of the State Department. The USIA represents the official
voice of the U.S. Government in presenting news on current

events and U.S. policies and programs to people in other nations. Its purpose is to influence public opinion in a way favorable to the United States and to counteract Communist or other propaganda. It also has the responsibility of advising the U.S. Government on implications of our policies and actions on foreign public opinion. Although there has been disagreement over the appropriateness of an "official" information agency and over some of its methods of operation, the influence of communications media on public opinion and the importance of public opinion in world affairs has led to fairly general acceptance of the need for "explaining" ourselves abroad.

The educational exchange programs under the State Department send U.S. students and teachers abroad and bring foreign nationals to the United States to promote cultural understanding and mutual educational benefit.

CONDUCT OF FOREIGN AFFAIRS

The conduct of foreign affairs was noted above as a responsibility without which a nation cannot truly call itself independent. Expenditures under this subfunction provide for this activity and are, largely, expended by the Department of State to represent the United States throughout the world (e.g., embassies, United Nations), for administration and, also, for participation in, and contributions to, international organizations. Another program under this subfunction is the Arms Control and Disarmament Agency (ACDA), which conducts research, is involved in international negotiations and international control systems, and publishes information related to arms control.

This completes discussion of the International Relations subfunctions, which add to the 1971 outlays, as shown in Table 28.

RESEARCH AND DEVELOPMENT

The minor importance of R&D in International Relations (in dollar terms) to either the overall field or R&D in general was noted earlier. Its rank in relation to R&D in other fields was eleven (out of twelve), and it was only 0.8 percent of all International Relations outlays. The figures are shown in Table 29. Program area descriptions, excerpted from The Budget, follow.

TABLE 28

International Relations Outlays by Subfunction, FY 1971
(In Millions of Dollars)

Subfunction	Dollars	Percent of Total
Economic and Financial Assistance	2,357	61.0
Food for Peace	852	22.1
Conduct of Foreign Affairs	412	10.7
Foreign Information and Exchange Activities	241	6.2
Subtotal	3,862	100.0
Adjustments	-273	
Total Outlays	3,589	

Source: The Budget, FY 1971, p. 91.

TABLE 29

International Relations R&D Conduct Expenditures
by Program Area, FY's 1969-71

1971 Rank	Program Area	1969[a]	1970[b]	1971[b]
1	Agency for International Development	9.0	18.7	22.5
2	Arms Control and Development Agency	4.6	4.2	3.4
3	Other State R&D	0.8	0.6	0.8
4	Peace Corps	0.3	0.7	0.5
5	United States Information Agency	0.2	0.1	0.3
	Total	14.9	24.3	27.5

[a]Actual.
[b]Estimate.

Source: Data obtained from the Office of Management and Budget.

Agency for International Development

The AID research unit conducts programs on the following: techniques for developing both the human and natural resources of the less developed countries, the adaptation of available technology to the conditions in those countries, and the nature of the relationship between economic and social change. Excluded is AID's technical assistance program, which is many times larger than the research program.

Arms Control and Disarmament Agency (ACDA)

External research and field testing are supported, with emphasis on the control, limitation, and reduction of strategic offensive and defensive weapons systems in support of bilateral negotiations on strategic arms limitations.

Other State

Other R&D is carried out in connection with the Department of State's responsibilities for the representation of the United States and its citizens abroad, political and economic negotiations and reporting, consular operations, and representation on international commissions.

Peace Corps

The Peace Corps provides trained Americans to interested countries in need of middle-level manpower and to promote understanding between the people of the United States and the peoples served. The Peace Corps conducts small amounts of research in connection with its overall objectives.

United States Information Agency

USIA conducts R&D in engineering development, equipment design, and radio propagation techniques applicable to the Voice of America.

NOTES

1. Executive Office of the President, Bureau of the Budget, The Budget in Brief, FY 1971 (Washington, D.C.: U.S. Government Printing Office, 1970), p. 33.

2. 1967 Messages, Congressional Quarterly Almanac (Washington, D.C.: Congressional Quarterly Service, 1967).

3. Harry S. Truman, Inaugural Address (Washington, D.C.: The White House, January 20, 1949).

4. Task Force on International Development, U.S. Foreign Assistance in the 1970's: A New Approach (Washington, D.C.: U.S. Government Printing Office, 1970).

11

HOUSING AND
COMMUNITY
DEVELOPMENT

THE FIELD AS A WHOLE

The functional field of Housing and Community Development includes programs designed to move toward "a decent
home and a suitable living environment for every American
family."[1] Programs are aimed at improving the viability of
urban communities by stimulating the economy; helping combat slums; and assisting special groups through grants, loans,
and insurance to state and local governments and to individuals
and organizations. The basic content of this functional field
is the same as is presented in The Budget, with a change made
to include veterans' housing programs.

The Federal Government's interest in housing began, as
so many Government programs have, in recognition of a de-
fense-related need: housing for employees of industries involved in military production during World War I.* The Government built a number of housing projects for wartime
employees, but sold these to private owners and got out of the
housing field after the war. The Depression was the next event
causing the Government, once again, to become involved in
the housing field, in an attempt to shore up the economy and
to save homeowners from defaulting on their mortgages. A
U. S. Housing Authority was set up in 1937 to provide loans for
low-income housing and slum clearance. Gradually, the

_____

*In the most general sense, Federal interest in community
development was present earlier, with the Homestead Act of
1877 and other laws designed to develop the country westward.
These laws were in the nature of incentives to encourage others
to develop the lands and settle there. Participation of the
Federal Government in housing and community development
began in a direct way during World War I.

Government's interest in housing began to be focused more
toward the public welfare aspects as it sought to help special
groups in the population, such as the poor or veterans. Although the original impetus for the Government's involvement
was defense related, the field of Housing and Community
Development (hereafter referred to as Housing) contributes
only in an indirect way to this goal. There are some expenditures for military housing, which have been included in the
National Security field. The Housing field does contribute quite
directly to two other supergoals--those of Public Welfare and
Economic Growth. This was recognized with the strong involvement begun during the Depression and expanded after
World War II.

The Government's role has been continually surrounded
by controversy, especially in those programs having to do with
deteriorating areas and housing for the poor and for minority
groups. This controversy over the Government's role has
slowed down action, even after it was authorized in various
legislative acts and has, many critics charge, resulted in a
housing program that has largely benefited the middle class
and has done little for urban poor people, who live mostly in
slums. Innovations and many recent suggestions are being
made in an attempt to remedy this situation, but the country
has a long way to go to implement the policy declared in the
Housing Act of 1949, parts of which have become the byword
for our housing aims:

> The Congress hereby declares that the general
> welfare and security of the Nation and the health
> and living standards of its people require housing
> production and related community development
> sufficient to remedy the serious housing shortage,
> the elimination of substandard and other inade-
> quate housing through the clearance of slums and
> blighted areas, and the realization as soon as
> feasible of the goal of a decent home and suitable
> living environment for every American family,
> thus contributing to the development and redevelop-
> ment of communities and to the advancement of
> the growth, wealth, and security of the Nation. [2]

A review of Presidential messages in 1960 (Eisenhower's
last year of office), 1961 (Kennedy's first year), and 1968
(Johnson's last year), offers some examples of the changing
attitude and approach to housing during the last decade.

In 1960:

> In meeting [urban problems] we must, if we value
> our historic freedoms, keep within the traditional
> framework of our Federal system with powers
> divided between the national and state governments
> . . . I do not doubt that our urban and other per-
> plexing problems can be solved in the traditional
> American method. In doing so, we must realize
> that nothing is really solved and ruinous tendencies
> are set in motion by yielding to the deceptive bait
> of the 'easy' Federal tax dollar.[3]

In 1961:

> Our policy for housing and community development
> must be directed toward the accomplishment of
> three basic national objectives:
>   First, to renew our cities and assure growth
> of our rapidly expanding metropolitan areas.
>   Second, to provide decent housing for all of
> our people.
>   Third, to encourage a prosperous and efficient
> construction industry as an essential component of
> general economic prosperity and growth.[4]

In 1968:

> Surely, a nation that can go to the moon can place
> a decent home within the reach of its families.[5]

And

> Our goal is to eliminate substandard housing in
> ten years.[6]

The Housing and Urban Development Act of 1968 has been
referred to as the most far-reaching legislation since the
Housing Act of 1949, which began the urban renewal program.
This Act sets forth an objective to fulfill the long-standing goal
of "a decent home and suitable living environment for every
American family" within a decade. This is to be accomplished
through the construction or rehabilitation of 26 million units
(6 million for low- and moderate-income families) over this
period. Annual reports, comparing progress made during

each year with that year's stated goals, are then to be presented
to Congress.   This is a rather clear demonstration of a desire
both to set goals and to measure their achievement.

Some major provisions of the 1968 Act are the following:

1. Home-ownership assistance for low- and moderate-income
families through interest rate subsidies so that families pay
only 20 percent of their income on loan retirement (but this
must be at least the equivalent of paying a 1 percent interest
rate)

2. Expansion of Federal Housing Administration activity for
low-income housing in areas such as insuring mortgages for
families who normally would not qualify but are certified by
HUD; insuring loans to organizations purchasing housing for
resale as low- or moderate-income housing

3. New subsidies for construction or rehabilitation of low-
income housing by nonprofit organizations

4. Guarantee of obligations issued by private developers of
new towns or communities and assistance with their water,
sewer, and open-space projects

5. Speeding up of urban renewal through neighborhood development programs on an annual basis and percentage requirements for low- and moderate-income housing

6. Transfer of the Federal National Mortgage Association
(FNMA) to private ownership under general regulation of HUD
and establishment of the Government National Mortgage Association (GNMA) for special assistance and management functions

7. Establishment of a National Housing Partnership for
Federally chartered, privately funded corporations to provide
low- and moderate-income housing

8. Provides Government reinsurance for companies insuring
buildings in riot areas, accompanied by a fair access to insurance requirements (FAIR) program to assure that businesses
can obtain insurance from those insurance companies the
Government has reinsured

9. A joint Federal-private venture to provide flood insurance
for homeowners

10. Continued authorization of rent supplement and Model
Cities programs.

This 1968 Housing Act is indicative of heightened interest
of the Government in Housing and Community Development as
an important element in stability and growth of cities and in
the importance of providing adequate housing for low-income
families, not only through the public housing program but also
by providing incentives to the private market to stimulate their

entry into low-income housing. Stress has also been placed,
in this law, on providing jobs for local citizens and contracts
for local businesses in the areas where construction or rehabilitation is to take place.

Because of the preponderance of loan, or loan-guarantee,
programs in the past as the Government's principal method of
operation in the field of Housing and Community Development,
the data over the 1961-71 period, shown in Table 2, gives a
rather distorted view of the Government's interest. First,
the nature of such operations leads to possible distortions in
data for an individual year, and second, the impact of an operation is not necessarily reflected by a "net lending" figure.
Since World War II, about one-fourth of all private nonfarm
housing units started have been assisted by Federal insurance
or guarantees. The data in Table 2 show relatively low (and
in a few cases minus) figures up to 1966. The minus figures
result when repayments of loans and/or sales of mortgages
exceed disbursements. Starting with 1966, the figures begin
to pick up, reflecting the addition of actual expenditure programs in this field, and in 1971, the outlays are 1.9 percent
of total Government outlays, a growth of +1.5 percent in percent of total over 1961. This placed Housing in ninth rather
than eleventh rank (out of twelve) in 1971, as compared with
1961. In percent growth between 1961 and 1971, this field was
first (+910 percent). Because of the difficulties in the yearly
figures for this field as a whole and the problems of comparing
the net outlays between years, the figures for the last three
years are reviewed below in more detail. The data in Table
30 summarize subfunctional outlays for 1969-71.

Of the total outlays over the past three years, expenditures
accounted for 50 percent, 77 percent, and 91 percent from
1969 through 1971 and net lending for 50 percent, 23 percent,
and 9 percent. It is the variable nature of the net lending
figures from year to year that makes comparisons over time
somewhat hazardous. The figures that are most susceptible
to analysis over time are the gross expenditure figures. The
total gross expenditure figures in Table 30 are $1,773 million
for 1969, $2,862 million for 1970, and $3,532 million for 1971.
This shows clear growth in expenditure programs--61 percent
between 1969 and 1970 and 28 percent between 1970 and 1971.

A review of the last three years, using Table 30 as a
basis, shows a little more clearly than the total outlays of
Table 2 the interests and funding of the Government. Two
points should be emphasized: (a) because of lending operations,
yearly figures can be distorted, and net figures in any case

TABLE 30

Housing and Community Development Outlays by Subfunction, FY's 1969-71
(In Millions of Dollars)

Subfunction	Dollars			Percent of Total		
	1969	1970	1971	1969	1970	1971
Expenditures:						
Low- and Moderate-Income Housing Aids	344	548	861	19.4	19.1	24.4
Community Planning and Administration	47	81	97	2.7	2.8	2.7
Community Environment	595	1,115	1,127	33.6	39.0	31.9
Community Facilities	102	163	202	5.8	5.7	5.7
Concentrated Community Development	686	956	1,244	38.7	33.4	35.2
Total Gross Expenditures	1,773	2,862	3,532	100.0	100.0	100.0
Maintenance of Housing Mortgage Market[a]	-737	-392	-362			
	1,036	2,470	3,170			
Adjustments	- 13	- <1	- <1			
Subtotal, Expenditures	1,023	2,470	3,170			
Net Lending:						
Low- and Moderate-Income Housing Aids	527	605	638			
Community Planning and Administration	<1	1	-1			
Community Environment	37	7	46			
Community Facilities	44	37	34			
Concentrated Community Development	-2	4	-2			
Maintenance of Housing Mortgage Market	433	85	-418			
Subtotal, Net Lending	1,039	738	297			
Total Outlays	2,063	3,208	3,466			

[a]Because most figures under this subfunction are negative (i.e., income from loan-guarantee premiums), these figures have not been included in the subtotal for purposes of percentaging.

Note: Figures may not add to totals because of rounding.

Source: Data compiled from The Budget, FY 1971, Table 14, pp. 571-83.

142

will not reflect the impact of the Government's mortgage support programs, and (b) despite the difficulty in making comparisons using these yearly totals, it is clear that a major
increase has taken place in the very recent past and is planned
to continue in FY 1971 in Government expenditures (as distinct
from net lending) in this field.

In terms of agency involvement and interest, most of the
subfunctions and programs described below are the responsibility of HUD, which was established in the Housing Act of
1965 and pulled together various Government entities that had
been in existence for many years.   The Declaration of Purpose
in this Act was that "the general welfare and security of the
Nation and the health and living standards of our people require,
as a matter of national purpose, sound development of the
Nation's communities and metropolitan areas in which the vast
majority of its people live and work."[7]   Table 31 provides the
details of subfunctional outlays for 1969-71.   Items in Table
31 that are not the responsibility of HUD are the Federal
Savings and Loan Insurance Corporation, VA housing programs,
and OEO programs.

LOW- AND MODERATE-INCOME HOUSING AIDS

One of the largest programs in this subfunction is low-rent
public housing.   Government participation in low-rent public
housing began with passage of the United States Housing Act
of 1937.   Under this program, local housing authorities are
set up to handle public housing in a specified area, obtain
loans from the Public Housing Administration for planning
purposes, and receive annual subsidies for operations to make
up the difference between their obligations (on bonds sold to
the public, for maintenance, and so forth) and the income received from rents, which are set at a low level to serve tenants
within specified low-income levels.

Public housing programs have never filled the need for
low-rental housing, and have been criticized from all direc-
tions--from those who feel the private market should take care
of housing or those who dislike public housing being used as a
vehicle for other objectives, such as integration, to those who
feel public housing has been inadequate in quantity, poor in
quality, and, at the same time, has contributed to "ghettoizing"
rather than dispersion of low-income residents throughout an
area.   New techniques have been instituted in the past few years
in an attempt to meet some of these criticisms.

TABLE 31

Housing and Community Development Outlay Details, FY's 1969-71
(In Millions of Dollars)

Program or Agency	Outlays		
	1969[a]	1970[b]	1971[b]
Low- and Moderate-Income Housing Aids (HUD):			
Homeownership Assistance	1	18	84
Rent Reduction Payments in Private Housing	5	20	59
Low-Rent Public Housing	352	457	646
Special Assistance Functions	432	546	617
Housing for the Elderly	76	49	29
Rehabilitation Loans and Other	6	63	63
Maintenance of the Housing Mortgage Market:			
Department of Housing and Urban Development:			
Mortgage insurance programs	-128	-196	-160
Management and liquidating functions	107	-109	-198
Guarantees of mortgage-backed securities and other	-47	3	c
Federal National Mortgage Association (trust)	-17	---	---
Fair housing and equal opportunity programs	2	6	11
Federal property insurance programs	-33	-19	-1
Federal Home Loan Bank Board and Other:			
Federal Savings and Loan Insurance Corporation and Other	-290	-154	-117
Veterans Housing (VA)	102	162	-315
Community Planning and Administration (HUD):			
Housing and Urban Research and Other	13	32	45
Comprehensive Planning and Training Programs	34	49	50
Community Environment (HUD):			
New Community Programs	---	-1	-1
Open-Space Land Programs	43	55	71
Urban Renewal Programs	589	1,068	1,104
Community Facilities (HUD):			
Water and Sewer Facility Grants	80	119	146
Public Facility Loans and Other	55	56	53
Neighborhood Facilities	11	26	38
Concentrated Community Development:			
Office of Economic Opportunity:			
Community action programs and other	668	660	712
Department of Housing and Urban Development:			
Model Cities program	15	300	530
Deductions for Offsetting Receipts:			
Interfund and Intragovernmental Transactions	-13	---	---
Proprietary Receipts from the Public	c	c	c
Total	2,063	3,208	3,466

[a]Actual.
[b]Estimate.
[c]Less than $0.5 million.
Note: Figures may not add to totals because of rounding.

Source: Edited excerpts from The Budget, FY 1971, p. 126.

144

Homeownership assistance subsidizes mortgage payments to enable lower-income families to keep payments at 20 percent of their income. Another program innovation has been the rent supplement program, under which the Government pays certain private housing groups the difference between the regular market rental value and the rental paid by the tenant, which is set at a certain percent of his income. The purpose of this program is to provide decent housing for families who often cannot, themselves, purchase such housing except at rates far in excess of 20 percent to 25 percent of their income, the generally accepted proportion of income that should be spent on housing. Another rental assistance program, for moderate-income families, attempts to provide them with housing for 25 percent of their income. The last line item on Table 31, rehabilitation loans, are made to help improve properties in deteriorating areas.

MAINTENANCE OF THE HOUSING MORTGAGE MARKET

This subfunction is oriented toward loan operations, and outlays are largely in the net lending rather than expenditure category. As Table 30 indicates, expenditures over the three fiscal years shown are negative, and net lending figures vary widely. Functions consist primarily of insuring and guaranteeing mortgages and savings and loan accounts. Premiums are charged to do this and, generally, exceed monies paid out for foreclosures--resulting in negative figures.

Government maintenance of the housing mortgage market started during the Depression, to stabilize the market and to make mortgages more available to potential homeowners by insuring or guaranteeing that 80 percent of the money borrowed would be returned to lenders, even if the owner defaulted on his payments. In order to protect their own investment, the Government charges a premium to insure loans and sets certain standards for houses financed by Government-insured loans. The GI Bill of 1944 established a similar system for veterans under the VA. Direct loans are also an element of this subfunction and are aimed at assisting veterans in financing homes.

COMMUNITY PLANNING AND ADMINISTRATION

The research program of HUD is included in this subfunction. The research program receiving major attention is
Operation Breakthrough, a program designed to demonstrate
the feasibility of volume production of housing, especially
lower-cost housing. New approaches will be tried in production, financing, marketing, management, and land use, and
HUD will absorb all costs above the market price of the prototype units constructed. Such volume production of housing may
be the only way to achieve the goal of 26 million units in a
decade, which was set forth by the Housing and Urban Development Act of 1968.
Comprehensive planning and training programs are financed
under this subfunction, with grants going to state, local, and
regional governments for them to fund studies that will help
in their decision-making and in training personnel. R&D program areas and expenditures are described later.

COMMUNITY ENVIRONMENT

Urban renewal was authorized under the Housing Act of
1949 as a slum clearance program. Expenditures under this
program have been substantial over the years but have come
under attack as being used to remove low-income (mainly
Negro) inhabitants of central cities and replacing their former
homes with high- and middle-income housing or with commercial buildings. Cities are often caught in the dilemma of want-
ing to bring more revenue-producing elements into the city
but having a responsibility not to force low-income residents
into another developing slum area. Legislation in 1968 authorized "neighborhood development programs," which are designed
to speed up urban renewal and which require that at least 20
percent of housing units in an urban renewal area be for low-
income tenants and at least 50 percent for low- and moderate-
income tenants combined.
Open-space land grants provide funds for comprehensive
community planning of an urban area with respect to parkland,
open spaces, and beautification.

COMMUNITY FACILITIES

Included here are grants for basic water and sewer facilities, loans for public facilities in areas where interest rates in the private market are very high, and grants for neighborhood centers to coordinate social services for disadvantaged residents in urban areas. Comprehensive planning is stressed in making these grants.

CONCENTRATED COMMUNITY DEVELOPMENT

Community Action programs make up about half of the total expenditures of the OEO. Established by the Economic Opportunity Act of 1964, OEO, through its Community Action programs, provides help for rural and urban communities to alleviate poverty by organizing and mobilizing their resources. Emphasis is placed on direct participation by the poor people, who are expected to benefit from the various projects, which range from literacy programs and vocational rehabilitation to legal and health services. OEO, through Community Action agencies, participates in the neighborhood centers mentioned earlier, in conjunction with HUD and other Government agencies.

The Model Cities program, a key element in the 1966 Housing Act, provides for planning and action grants for cities to establish areas of their jurisdiction, in which an all-out attempt is to be made to rehabilitate blighted areas, coordinating activities in health, education, welfare, manpower, recreation, transportation, and physical rehabilitation, and to develop the area as a whole rather than through piecemeal approaches.

RESEARCH AND DEVELOPMENT

Table 3 shows no R&D reported in the field of Housing and Community Development in 1961. In 1971, R&D expenditures are expected to rise to $73 million, as shown in Table 32. This places R&D in this field ninth in rank (out of twelve) in 1971, and it amounted to 0.5 percent of all Government R&D outlays. As a percent of the Housing and Community Development field, R&D is only 2.1 percent, although its recent growth has shown an increasing interest in R&D.

TABLE 32

Housing and Community Development R&D Conduct
Expenditures by Program Area, FY's 1969-71
(In Millions of Dollars)

1971 Rank	Program Areas	1969[a]	1970[b]	1971[b]
1	Office of Economic Opportunity[c]	28.3	18.5	37.0
2	Urban Research and Technology (HUD)	6.6	13.6	23.5
3	Other Housing and Community Development R&D	5.1	8.3	11.3
4	Low-Income Housing (HUD)	1.4	1.4	1.5
		41.4	41.8	73.3

[a]Actual.
[b]Estimate.
[c]One-half of total.

Source: Data obtained from The Department of Housing and Urban Development and the Office of Management and Budget.

Urban Research and Technology*

This program area funds research in housing, urban technology, metropolitan growth, and urban problems. Other
major areas of emphasis are improving public facilities and
services, gathering data on housing and mortgage markets,
applying university resources to urban problems, and improving
state and local government procedures and methods for dealing
with urban problems.

Through Operation Breakthrough, HUD develops and tests
innovations in housing design, construction, financing, and
marketing, with considerable attention to community environment. One of the objectives of this program is to develop a
self-sustained mechanism for providing volume production of
marketable housing at stable or reduced costs for all income
groups, particularly those groups that have had difficulty in
obtaining satisfactory housing in the past.

Low-Income Housing Demonstration Programs

Grants to public or private bodies or agencies to develop
and demonstrate new or improved means of providing housing
for low-income persons and families, including handicapped
families, are authorized by the Housing Act of 1961.** Demonstration projects under this program test new approaches in
construction design and methods to lower construction costs,
new or improved ways of rehabilitating and upgrading sound
but deficient structures, means of facilitating home ownership
by low-income families, and ways of providing technical advice
and assistance to nonprofit sponsors of low- and moderate-
income housing.

Office of Economic Opportunity

OEO's research and pilot projects are designed to serve
as the basis for planning programs for alleviating poverty and
promoting equality of opportunity. This includes identification
of need, design of experimental projects, the conduct and
evaluation of social experiments, expansion of successful

---

*Descriptions of these program areas are excerpted from
The Budget.
**42 U.S.C. 1436, as amended.

experimental efforts to pilot scale, and development of mechanisms for moving these programs to full-scale operation,
either within the agency or to other organizations.

NOTES

1. Housing Act of 1949, Public Law 81-171 (Washington,
D.C., U.S. Government Printing Office, July 15, 1949).

2. Ibid.

3. Dwight D. Eisenhower, State of the Union Message
(Washington, D.C.: The White House, 1960).

4. John F. Kennedy, Housing and Community Development
Message (Washington, D.C.: The White House, 1961).

5. Lyndon B. Johnson, State of the Union Message
(Washington, D.C.: The White House, 1968).

6. Lyndon B. Johnson, Economic Report of the President
(Washington, D.C.: U.S. Government Printing Office, 1968),
p. 21.

7. Housing Act of 1965, Public Law 89-174, September
9, 1965.

CHAPTER **12** NATURAL RESOURCES

THE FIELD AS A WHOLE

The functional field of Natural Resources in The Budget
includes programs for the conservation, development, and improvement of mineral and other land resources; water quality
and supply; forests, fish, and wildlife; and recreational areas.
This categorization has been modified to include the nonmilitary
activities of the AEC and to exclude the Federal Water Quality
Administration, which has been placed in the Environment
field.

The area of natural resources has been an area of long-
standing concern to the Federal Government in its desire,
originally, to encourage expansion of settlement across the
continent and, more recently, to conserve resources. The
field of Natural Resources contributes primarily to the supergoal of Economic Development, as, for example, in provision
of energy supplies vital to almost every industry in our economy
or of the water supply necessary for irrigation and industry.
It also contributes secondarily, but in crucial respects, to
National Security, as evidenced by the periodic concern over
strategic stockpiles to reduce dependence on foreign supplies
of various raw materials vital to defense.

The allocation of Government funds to this functional field
shows that, relative to other areas of Government interest,
Natural Resources has not been among the more favored fields
in the 1960's. Table 2 shows outlays for the Natural Resources
field from 1961 to 1971 and the percent of total for each year.
The highest percent was 2.9 percent in 1961, and, since then,
there has been a decrease to 1.5 percent--a decline of 1.4
percent. This occurred, despite a slight growth in actual outlays from $2.7 billion to $2.9 billion, because other fields
were growing much faster. In allocation by fields, Natural
Resources ranked tenth (out of twelve) in 1971, down from
sixth in 1961.

From the standpoint of R&D, Natural Resources presents

a much different picture. When R&D conduct expenditures are examined, Natural Resources is in a stronger relative position in rank of R&D monies and in importance to the field. For example, although only tenth in rank for the whole field among other fields, Natural Resources ranks fifth in importance in 1971 R&D--down, however, from second in 1961. Natural Resources R&D, then, is still among the more important fields for R&D funds, though its position relative to other fields has slipped in total outlays.

In importance of R&D to its respective functional field, Natural Resources also ranks high--and R&D has been of increasing importance to the field over the 1961-71 period. In 1961, R&D conduct expenditures accounted for 19 percent of all Natural Resources expenditures, which placed it third in terms of importance of R&D to the field. In 1971, estimated R&D conduct expenditures comprise 25 percent of all Natural Resources expenditures, placing it second in importance of R&D to the field.

A more detailed look at overall outlays for Natural Resources appears in Table 33, which shows the actual 1969, and estimated 1970 and 1971, outlays as given in The Budget, broken down by subfunctions and by areas under these subfunctions.

A glance at Table 33 shows that the Interior Department has the widest interest in the Natural Resources field, with responsibility for most of the line items appearing in the Table. But in outlays, the Army (Corps of Engineers) is not far behind, though its interests are not as diverse as those of the Interior Department. The AEC, the Agriculture Department (Forest Service and Soil Conservation Service), and the TVA also have important responsibilities in this field. Total outlays for 1971, by major agency, for Natural Resources are indicated below in Table 34.

A special point to note in this field is the high negative amounts under proprietary receipts from the public, which are receipts from such activities as offshore oil leases, leasing mineral lands, selling power and timber, and disposal of public lands. Receipts from such sources are expected to go down as the Government reduces public land sales and reduces offshore oil leases because of oil leakage problems.

The following sections will treat the elements that make up the Natural Resources field more fully in terms of objectives, policy, and programs. The areas discussed will be Water Resources and Power, Nuclear Energy, Land Management, Mineral Resources, Recreational Resources, and Other Natural Resources Programs.

TABLE 33

Natural Resources Outlay Details, FY's 1969-71
(In Millions of Dollars)

Program or Agency	Outlays		
	1969[a]	1970[b]	1971[b]
Water Resources and Power:			
Corps of Engineers (Army)[c]	1,244	1,235	1,395
Department of the Interior:			
Bureau of Reclamation[c]	288	274	326
Power marketing agencies[c]	140	136	131
Office of Saline Water[c]	37	37	28
Office of Water Resources Research and other	11	10	11
Tennessee Valley Authority	187	224	425
Soil Conservation Service--Watershed Projects (Agriculture)[c]	101	123	124
International Boundary and Water Commission (State)	12	4	8
Federal Power Commission and Other[c]	21	25	28
Total, Water Resources and Power	2,041	2,067	2,475
Nuclear Energy (AEC)	862	864	844
Land Management:			
Forest Service (Agriculture)[c]	473	549	590
Bureau of Land Management and Other (Interior)[c]	170	196	180
Mineral Resources (Interior)[c]	71	116	110
Recreational Resources (Interior):			
Bureau of Outdoor Recreation:			
Present programs[c]	129	180	193
Further program proposals	---	7	62
National Park Service[c]	133	147	151
Bureau of Sport Fisheries and Wildlife and Other[c]	109	112	139
Other Natural Resources Programs (Interior):			
Geological Survey	92	98	105
Bureau of Commercial Fisheries and Other[c]	69	80	78
Deductions for Offsetting Receipts:			
Interfund and Intragovernmental Transactions	[d]	-1	-1
Proprietary Receipts from the Public	-1,372	-1,324	-2,047
Total	2,776	3,091	2,882

[a]Actual.
[b]Estimate.
[c]Includes both Federal funds and trust funds.
[d]Less than $500,000.
Note: Figures may not add to totals because of rounding.

Source: Edited excerpts from The Budget, FY 1971, p. 109.

TABLE 34

Natural Resources Outlays by Agency, FY 1971
(In Millions of Dollars)

Agency	Dollars	Percent of Total
Department of the Interior	1,512	30.7
Army	1,395	28.3
Atomic Energy Commission	844	17.1
Department of Agriculture	714	14.5
Tennessee Valley Authority	425	8.6
Other	38	0.8
Total Gross Expenditures	4,930	100.0
Proprietary Receipts from Public	-2,048	
Total Outlays	2,882	

Note: Figures may not add to totals because of rounding.

Source: Data compiled from The Budget, FY 1971, Table 14, pp. 571-83.

WATER RESOURCES AND POWER

The largest subfunction in the Natural Resources field is water resources and power, which involves a number of activities in the Interior Department, the Army Corps of Engineers, TVA, the Soil Conservation Service of Agriculture, and a few others. The Federal Government is interested in water for irrigation, industrial, and general public use, and as a source of power. It has financed water projects and extensive construction to satisfy these needs. Increasing competition among various user groups for fresh water has changed water from its prior status as a freely available resource and has increased emphasis on multiple-purpose projects and more comprehensive management of the water supply. Research has been an important element in attempts to conserve water supplies and in creating new sources of supply through conversion of salt water or brackish water to fresh water.

Whereas the Eisenhower Administration placed emphasis on local, rather than Federal, action in water resources and power problems and, particularly, in the construction of water and power projects, the Kennedy Administration moved toward a much more active Federal role in such projects and in creating more public power systems and nonprofit rural electric cooperatives. Increased emphasis was placed on multipurpose projects and development of comprehensive plans for major river systems. In 1964, the Water Resources Research Act was passed to help in using existing supplies to best advantage. A non-Federal National Water Commission was established in 1968 to review U.S. water resource problems, including more efficient use of water, reduction of pollution, desalinization, weather modification, and economic and social consequences of water resource development.

The saline water program was started in 1952, with expansions to the research program being added in 1955 and 1961. In 1958, legislation was enacted, authorizing the construction of five Federal demonstration plants, two to convert brackish water and three to convert sea water. Each plant was to use a different method of conversion. In 1967, Congress authorized the Interior Department to participate, along with the AEC and a few private utilities, in construction of a nuclear power and water desalting plant in California. The Office of Science and Technology, in 1964, predicted that, with a strong R&D program, it would be possible, by about 1975, to build combined nuclear energy power and saline water conversion plants at a cost low enough to make saline water conversion an economic possibility for use as municipal water supply.

The TVA, established amid controversy in 1933, has remained controversial, especially in relation to its function in the electrical power field. TVA had been established to help improve the economy of the region by supplying low-cost electricity, improving farming and forestry, and controlling floods. Controversy has continued, as TVA has expanded its generating facilities, as to whether TVA or privately owned public utilities should meet new power requirements of the area. Although TVA has been a favorite object of attack, the objective of carrying out a comprehensive development program for the area continues.

Expenditures by the Army Corps of Engineers, largely for construction projects, make up over half of the expenditures for this subfunction and are related to activities such as flood control, water supply, and hydroelectric power.

NUCLEAR ENERGY

After World War II, the Army Manhattan District began
studies on nuclear reactors for nonweapons use. This work
was extended by the AEC after its creation in 1946 and has
continued ever since. The Atomic Energy Act of 1954 enabled
private industry, under AEC licenses, to build and operate
nuclear power plants, designed ultimately to foster the development of commercially competitive, electricity using nuclear
reactors. In 1955, the Cooperative Power Demonstration
Reactor Program was initiated, providing Federal aid for such
demonstration plants by private industry. A twelve-year
development program was announced by AEC in 1962. The
aim was to make nuclear electric power commercially feasible
in high-cost power areas by 1968 and, in most areas, during
the 1970's and to make the use of breeder reactors commercially feasible in the 1980's. The thought was that, by the
year 2000, nuclear power would supply about half the country's
needs for electricity, at the same time that increasing demands
would still keep conventional fuels commercially competitive.
Because conventional sources of fuel are ultimately of limited
quantity and nuclear fuels almost unlimited, the Government
has moved ahead since World War II to develop this resource.
But, in the short run, it may create serious problems of adjustment in the other fuel industries. This has led to continuing
debate and rancor over the Government's role. As nuclear
energy has moved toward commercial feasibility, various steps
have been taken or are contemplated to reduce dependence on
Government support. In 1964, legislation was passed requiring
nuclear-electric power plants to purchase nuclear fuels at a
fair market rate rather than leasing them at low rates from
the AEC. Legislation is currently under consideration that
would end reactor-building under R&D licenses and require
that all licenses come under commercial rules.

LAND MANAGEMENT

Expenditures under this subfunction are partly those of
the Forest Service in the Department of Agriculture, which is
responsible for management and use of the 187 million acres
of national forests and grasslands, for forestry research, and
for advice and help toward good management and use of privately

owned forest resources.   Policy, as with many other natural
resources, centers on multiple-use and sustained yield.

About 280 million acres of Federally owned land are set
aside for special uses, such as national parks and forests and
military bases.   Other Federally owned lands, about 490
million acres, largely located in the West and in Alaska, are
considered as "the public lands," administered by the Bureau
of Land Management.   Although Federal policy once emphasized
disposal of these lands to individuals or to state and local
governments, present policy emphasizes retention for public
needs and use, multiple-use where possible, and management
of resources on these lands to sustain or increase their yields.
In 1964, Congress set up a Public Land Law Review Commission to recommend national policy on public land management
and disposal.   The final report of this Commission, submitted
in 1970, recommended sweeping changes in the many laws
dealing with public land and extensive adjustments in administrative procedures and responsibility.

MINERAL RESOURCES

Although expenditures in this subfunction (by the Bureau
of Mines and the Bureau of Land Management) are less than
those of the other subfunctions already discussed, this is
largely because the Federal Government has less direct responsibility for development of these resources, which are
nonrenewable and are exploited by private industry.   The importance of mineral resources to the national economy and
security, however, is far greater than these relative expenditures would indicate, and the Government has a large stake in
their development and utilization.   One of the major objectives
with regard to mineral resources (including fuels--oil, coal,
gas--metals, and other nonfuel minerals) is maintenance of
an adequate supply that is economically feasible to exploit.
This objective has been pursued through research and exploration, subsidies, stockpiling, market control, and management
practices on Federal lands.

Concern over "using up" the nation's mineral resources
has existed for many years, partly allayed by availability of
foreign supplies, discovery of new supplies, better techniques
for extraction and use, substitutability of other minerals and
materials, and more efficient processes.   But, with growing
population and expanding industrial needs, the maintenance of

adequate supplies at reasonable cost is a continuing concern
of the Government over the long-term. In the short-term, a
recent problem has been just the reverse--oversupply of many
minerals, especially as overseas supplies were developed,
creating difficult market conditions for domestic suppliers.
This has created policy conflicts because of the desire to maintain a strong domestic minerals industry as well as the desire
to lower trade barriers and conserve domestic resources.

On the fuels side of mineral resources, the major policy
problem has been to find a suitable role for the Government in
this very competitive field. The Government is interested in
maintaining multiple sources for energy, without directly in-
tervening in the market. This has placed it in a difficult position between the various fuel industries, first as oil and gas
began to overtake coal as a source of energy and, more recently as nuclear energy developed, largely with Government
R&D funds, promises to take a major share of future power
production.

RECREATIONAL RESOURCES

The National Park Service, the Bureau of Outdoor Recreation, and the Bureau of Sport Fisheries and Wildlife, all in
the Department of the Interior, make up this subfunction.
The National Park System, consisting of more than 25 million
acres of land, has the objectives of preserving areas of special
natural beauty or interest, of historical importance, or for
outdoor recreation. Since the creation of Yellowstone in 1872,
it has been a principle of park management that commercial
exploitation is generally excluded from the park system.

The Bureau of Outdoor Recreation was established by law
in 1963 in recognition of the need for planning of future recreational needs and resources. It has the responsibility of formulating and maintaining a comprehensive plan for outdoor recreation development by all levels of government. In response
to the growing population and rising pressures on available
outdoor recreational facilities, the Government has further
developed the policy of multiple-use of Government lands to
include recreation, and it has attempted to acquire undeveloped
areas for preservation for the future. The Bureau of Sport
Fisheries and Wildlife is responsible for conserving sport
fishery and wildlife resources and for developing a national
program for their use.

OTHER NATURAL RESOURCE PROGRAMS

The Geological Survey was established in 1879 to provide
for the "classification of the public lands and the examination
of the geological structure, mineral resources, and products
of the national domain."[1] In 1962, this was expanded to allow
investigations outside the national domain.

The function of the Bureau of Commercial Fisheries is to
strengthen the fishing industry and conserve fishery resources.
Problems requiring legislative action since World War II have
included threats to fishery resources from pollution, pesticides,
and water project construction and competitive decline of the
U.S. fishing fleet. Research has grown in its contribution to
the solution of many of the problems involved.

This completes description of some of the activities,
legislation, and policy in the Natural Resources functional
field. Estimated 1971 outlays for the subfunctions discussed,
before exclusion of adjustments, are shown in Table 35.

TABLE 35

Natural Resources Outlays by Subfunction, FY 1971
(In Millions of Dollars)

Subfunction	Dollars	Percent of Total
Water Resources and Power	2,475	50.2
Nuclear Energy	844	17.1
Land Management	771	15.6
Recreational Resources	546	11.1
Other Natural Resources Programs	183	3.7
Mineral Resources	110	2.2
	4,930	100.0
Adjustments	-2,048	
Total Outlays	2,882	

Note: Figures may not add to totals because of rounding.

Source: The Budget, FY 1971, p. 109.

RESEARCH AND DEVELOPMENT

As noted in the beginning of this chapter, R&D has been in a stronger relative position in this field vis-à-vis other fields than has the overall field. In R&D, Natural Resources ranks fifth in importance, as opposed to tenth for the field as a whole in 1971. However, the relative position of each has fallen since 1961. It was also noted earlier that R&D ranks high in importance in terms of percent of total outlays in the field of Natural Resources, comprising 25 percent of all expenditures in 1971, second in importance only to Space. Table 36 shows the various program areas of R&D in Natural Resources and their estimated 1969-71 R&D conduct expenditures.

If the R&D program areas are combined according to the subfunctions, the relationship shown in Table 37 emerges.

Because of differences in relative importance of R&D to each subfunction, this distribution is very different from the total outlay distribution by subfunction. Obvious examples of the differences are the large portion of R&D in the nuclear energy program (62 percent) and, by contrast, the large portion of construction and maintenance outlays in the water resources programs.

Department of the Interior*

Geological Survey

The research program in this area is directed toward better understanding and interpretation of the configuration, composition, and properties of the earth's crust through topographical survey and mapping, resources survey and mapping, marine geology and hydrology, water resources investigation, conservation of soil and moisture, land and minerals, and other information necessary for the intelligent exploration for, and utilization of, the nation's natural resources. Increased attention is being focused on research dealing with geologic hazards in rapidly developing urban areas. Emphasis is also being placed on environmental data programs and environmental planning generally.

---

*Descriptions of Natural Resources R&D program areas are excerpted from The Budget.

TABLE 36

Natural Resources R&D Conduct Expenditures by Program Area, FY's 1969-71

(In Millions of Dollars)

1971 Rank	Program Area	Agency	1969[a]	1970[b]	1971[b]
1	Reactor Development	AEC	443.0	424.0	432.0
2	Bureau of Mines	Interior	36.2	44.0	57.3
3	Fish and Wildlife	Interior	46.8	49.6	52.2
4	Forest Service	Agriculture	40.6	43.3	47.7
5	Geological Survey	Interior	35.2	39.4	40.5
6	Office of Saline Water	Interior	25.9	25.9	22.3
7	Other Interior R&D	Interior	10.4	12.7	14.3
8	Civil Functions	DOD	8.8	10.3	11.8
9	Other Atomic Energy Commission R&D	AEC	12.5	13.0	10.5
10	Office of Water Resources Research	Interior	10.8	9.8	10.4
11	Office of Coal Research	Interior	7.4	5.2	9.9
12	Tennessee Valley Authority R&D	TVA	3.7	4.3	4.6
	Total		681.3	681.3	713.5

[a]Actual.

[b]Estimate.

Note: Figures may not add to totals because of rounding.

Source: Data obtained from The Budget, FY 1971, the Department of the Interior, the Department of Agriculture, the Department of Defense, and the Tennessee Valley Authority.

TABLE 37

Natural Resources R&D Conduct Expenditures
by Subfunction, FY 1971

Subfunction	Percent of Total
Water Resources and Power	7. 6
Nuclear Energy	62. 0
Land Management	7. 3
Mineral Resources	9. 4
Recreational Resources	2. 9
Other Natural Resources Programs	10. 8
Total	100. 0

Source: Data obtained from The Budget, FY 1971, the
Department of the Interior, the Department of Agriculture,
the Department of Defense, and the Tennessee Valley
Authority.

Bureau of Mines

The research program of this Bureau is concerned with
conserving, evaluating, and developing mineral resources.
Areas of interest are coal, petroleum, oil shale, metallurgy,
mining, marine mineral mining, and explosives. Under these
areas, attention is directed toward the problems of safety
hazards and pollution aspects.

Office of Coal Research

This agency is responsible for research programs on new
and more efficient methods of mining, preparing, and utilizing
coal and coordination of research with recognized interested
groups.

Office of Saline Water

This agency funds R&D on processes for converting saline
water to fresh water in quality suitable for municipal, industrial, and agricultural uses.

Office of Water Resources Research

The objectives of research in this area are to stimulate
and sponsor programs in the fields of water--and of resources
that affect water--and to assist in assuring the nation at all
times a supply of water, sufficient in quantity and quality, to
meet the requirements of its expanding population.

Other Departments of the Interior

Other research programs are conducted by the Bonneville
Power Administration, Bureau of Land Management, Bureau
of Outdoor Recreation, National Park Service, and the Bureau
of Reclamation.

Atomic Energy Commission

Reactor Development

Research in this area includes the development of nuclear
power reactors for central station applications and the development of power and propulsion reactors for a variety of civilian
and space applications, together with R&D on reactor technology
and nuclear safety.

The emphasis of the civilian power reactor category is
now directed to the development of the fast breeder reactor,
which promises to produce more fissionable nuclear fuel than
is consumed in the process of producing power. R&D continues
on advanced converter and thermal breeder power reactors
and on the application of nuclear power to desalting and other
processes.

Other AEC

These consist of isotopes development and civilian application of nuclear explosives. Isotopes development promotes
and encourages new uses of radioisotopes and radiation technology; radiation preservation of foods; heat sources for potential applications, including a circulatory support system
(nuclear-powered artificial heart); and isotopic measuring and
diagnostic systems for tracing and analyzing environmental
pollution. Civilian application of nuclear explosives (PLOW-
SHARE) provides for the investigation, development, and
demonstration of peaceful uses for nuclear explosives, with

R&D aimed at a fundamental understanding of nuclear explosive design and explosion phenomenology and its application.

Other Agencies

Tennessee Valley Authority

This agency conducts scientific R&D activities under its responsibilities to aid in the unified development of the region, develop and test new or improved chemical fertilizers, and improve the efficiency of its operations. In cooperation with the Public Health Service, TVA conducts research on economic disposal of solid wastes. Studies are also directed toward the potential effect of natural resource use and industrial and urban development on the environment to prevent its degradation and to enhance its quality.

Civil Functions (DOD)

These include coastal engineering R&D studies that deal with physical phenomena, techniques, basic principles, and remedial or control measures related to shore protection and improvement. Civil works investigations are also made to improve procedures for analysis of hydrologic and engineering data, design methods, better materials and practices for the construction and maintenance of hydraulic structures, and improved procedures used in formulating plans for water resources development. A joint research program is carried out with the AEC on nuclear explosives for civil construction.

Forest Service (Department of Agriculture)

This agency conducts research programs, including forest and range management studies, forest fire protection, pest and disease control, forest products, and engineering and forest resource economics.

NOTES

1. Act establishing U.S. Geological Survey, 20 Stat. 394; 43 U.S.C. 31, March 3, 1879, quoted in U.S. Government Organization Manual, 1968-1969 (Washington, D.C.: U.S. Government Printing Office, 1968), p. 257.

CHAPTER **13** SPACE

THE FIELD AS A WHOLE

The functional field of Space includes programs designed
"to improve our ability to operate in the space environment,
advance man's knowledge of the universe, and use the experience gained for man's benefit."[1] The Budget includes all of
NASA's expenditures in this field, and only those of NASA. In
keeping with the goal-oriented conceptual framework of this
book, this categorization has been modified to exclude two
areas of NASA work that seem to fit more appropriately into
other functional fields. Thus, Space science has been transferred to the Education, Knowledge, and Manpower field and
Aviation technology has been transferred to the functional field
of Commerce, Transportation, and Communications. The
field of Space remaining includes NASA's program areas of
manned space flight, space applications, space technology,
and supporting space activities.

The development of the various space applications technologies is considered to support the Space functional field.
However, as operational space applications systems evolve
in other fields, such as Natural Resources; Environment;
Agriculture and Rural Development; and Commerce, Transportation, and Communications, consideration should be given
to including such budget outlays under the field of use.

There is a significant amount of space work being carried
out by DOD, but the direct reason for this work is the further-
ance of the national security, and, therefore, this element is
included under the National Security field. Space activities of
a few other agencies (e. g. , Environmental Science Services
Administration) are included in the field of use (i. e. , Environment).

Although a small amount of space research was being
pursued through the DOD Vanguard project prior to the fall
of 1957, it was not until the launching of Sputnik by the U. S. S. R.
on October 4, 1957, that a real impetus was given to exploration

of space by the United States. The worldwide reaction seemed
to mark it in the public's eye as a spectacular achievement
(even beyond its technological value), and to many people in the
United States, it signified that the United States was "second
best." The reaction to this possible situation resulted in a
questioning of the nation's capabilities, its system of science
education, and its position in the eyes of the world. Although
there was no clear military use for a Sputnik, there were fears
that the Soviet Union was surpassing the United States in rocket-
ry and other areas of science and technology, leading, poten-
tially, to military advantage. During the next half year, various spokesmen in the Government (Executive and Congressional),
as well as scientists and engineers outside the Government,
presented their views on how best to meet the Soviet challenge
to U.S. supremacy.

The end result was the establishment of a civilian space
agency--NASA--to pursue peaceful activities in space, while
activities primarily concerned with defense were to be the
responsibility of DOD. The objective of space activities were
set out in Section 102.(c) of the enabling legislation:

(c) The aeronautical and space activities of the
United States shall be conducted so as to contribute materially to one or more of the following objectives:
(1) The expansion of human knowledge of
phenomena in atmosphere and space;
(2) The improvement of the usefulness,
performance, speed, safety, and efficiency of
aeronautical and space vehicles;
(3) The development and operation of vehicles
capable of carrying instruments, equipment, supplies, and living organisms through space;
(4) The establishment of long-range studies
of the potential benefits to be gained from, the opportunities for, and the problems involved in the
utilization of aeronautical and space activities for
peaceful and scientific purposes;
(5) The preservation of the role of the United
States as a leader in aeronautical and space science
and technology and in the application thereof to the
conduct of peaceful activities within and outside the
atmosphere;
(6) The making available to agencies directly
concerned with national defense of discoveries that

have military value or significance, and the furnish-
ing by such agencies, to the civilian agency established to direct and control nonmilitary aeronautical
and space activities, of information as to discoveries which have value or significance to that agency;

(7) Cooperation by the United States with other
nations and groups of nations in work done pursuant
to this Act and in the peaceful application of the results thereof; and

(8) The most effective utilization of the scientific and engineering resources of the United States,
with close cooperation among all interested agencies of the United States in order to avoid unneces-
sary duplication of effort, facilities, and equipment. [2]

In its relation to the supergoals identified in Chapter 1,
the field of Space most clearly and directly relates to the supergoal of National Security and International Relations. Even
though the aspects of direct concern to defense are handled
by DOD, the international prestige and competition element
that was so important in the establishment of NASA falls under
the same supergoal. Although the work of NASA has contributed importantly to the field of Education, Knowledge, and
Manpower and, thereby, indirectly to the supergoals of Economic Development and Public Welfare, these goals are over-
shadowed by the ultimate aim of "the preservation of the role
of the United States as a leader . . . "[3]

President Kennedy, in 1961, stated his belief that "this
nation should commit itself to achieving the goal, before this
decade is out, of landing a man on the moon and returning him
safely to the earth."[4] He indicated that efforts in space were
not merely a race: "Space is open to us now; and our eager-
ness to share its meaning is not governed by the efforts of
others. We go into space because whatever mankind must
undertake, free men must fully share."[5] Although the United
States took up the gauntlet and achieved the goal of reaching
the moon, the image of space activities seems to have lost
some of the luster it had at the time of President Kennedy's
message in 1961.

President Johnson's 1968 Budget message spoke of space
achievements in a sober tone, stressing that "to meet our most
urgent national needs in some areas requires us to reduce
spending in others."[6] President Nixon's 1970 Budget message
stated: "Consistent with other national priorities, we shall

seek to extend our capability in space . . . "[7] But he then
notes that this will be done with smaller outlays.

The allocation of Government funds to this functional field
(as shown in Table 2) shows outlays rising from less than $0.5
billion in 1961 to a high of $5.2 billion in 1966 and falling, in
subsequent years, to an estimated $2.8 billion in 1971. Space
has risen from 0.5 percent of Government outlays in 1961 to
a high of 4.1 percent in 1966, and it is down to 1.5 percent in
1971. In allocation by fields, Space ranked eleventh (out of
twelve) in 1971, down from fifth place in 1966.

The R&D picture in Space is very different, because almost all work funded by NASA is classified as R&D. In R&D
expenditures, Space ranked fourth (out of twelve) in 1961, despite its rank near the bottom in overall outlays; it rose to
second place in R&D in 1962 and has remained in second place
since. Its R&D expenditures were 4.5 percent of all Government R&D expenditures in 1961, and this percentage had risen
to 30.9 percent by 1966 but fell to 18.1 percent in 1971. This
makes it one of the two most important in R&D funding (together
with DOD), for no other field funds as much as 10 percent of
total R&D expenditures.

In importance of R&D to its respective field, Space is
unique in having R&D comprise almost all of its total outlays--
86 percent in 1961 and 98 percent in 1971. Though this definition may be questioned as not being an accurate reflection
of the work performed, these are the figures as derived from
The Budget. This puts Space highest in terms of importance
of R&D to the field.

A more detailed look at overall outlays for Space appears
in Table 38, which shows the actual 1969, and estimated 1970
and 1971, outlays, as given in The Budget, broken down by
line items included. As was noted earlier, NASA is the only
agency having control of outlays under this field, as defined
here.

The following subsections will treat the elements that
make up the Space field in terms of programs and objectives.
The areas discussed will be manned space flight, space applications, space technology, and supporting space activities.
Because 98 percent of 1971 outlays are for R&D, the excerpted
Budget descriptions appearing in the R&D sections in other
chapters will make up the bulk of the material presented below.

TABLE 38

Space Outlay Details, FY's 1969-71
(In Millions of Dollars)

Program Area	Agency	Outlays		
		1969[a]	1970[b]	1971[b]
Manned Space Flight	NASA	2,781	2,355	1,937
Space Applications	NASA	113	155	161
Space Technology	NASA	344	337	306
Supporting Space Activities[a]NASA		390	387	376
Proprietary Receipts from the Public		- 6	- 6	- 15
Total		3,623	3,227	2,765

[a]Actual
[b]Estimate
[c]Includes both Federal funds and trust funds.
Note: Figures may not add to totals because of rounding.

Source: Edited excerpts from The Budget, FY 1971, p. 98.

MANNED SPACE FLIGHT

The largest element of the Space field is manned space flight, which is estimated in 1971 to account for 70 percent of Space outlays, as defined in this functional field. The dominance of this part of the Space field is a result of the goal (quoted above) that was set in the State of the Union Message delivered by President Kennedy to Congress in May, 1961. This objective of a manned lunar landing, though questioned by some at the time, was overwhelmingly accepted as the foremost space goal and was, during the past decade, the dominant articulated aim of our efforts in space.

The objective set forth by President Kennedy emerged as the Apollo program (following completion of Mercury and Gemini programs), which was set back, early in 1967, by the spacecraft fire but which recovered momentum and achieved success with the spectacular manned landing on the moon in 1969. The difficulty experienced in the Apollo 13 flight has caused some delay and renewed questioning of this program.

One of the difficulties of having had such a specific and over-riding goal arises with questions concerning the next steps to follow achievement of that goal. Although the enabling legislation set eight objectives for space activities, it has proved difficult to fall back on these generalized objectives after the publicity and exertion that went into the "hot pursuit" of the single objective that galvanized the country for most of a decade.

The estimates for this activity include the Apollo, Apollo Applications, and advanced mission studies programs. Funding provides for all NASA manned space-flight missions and the development of the required space vehicles and the study of advanced manned missions. The basic objective of the manned space-flight program is to develop and provide a national capability for manned operations in space that will achieve and maintain a position of leadership for the United States.

Apollo

The moon landing of the Apollo program provided the initial basis for an understanding of the moon and its relationship to the earth and the solar system. The moon affords an unequaled opportunity to study the formative processes of the solar system without the obliterating consequences of terrestrial erosion. Data from this source will be sought to provide a better understanding of the evolutionary history of earth and the dynamic processes that continue to transform it.

Apollo Applications

The Apollo Applications effort commences manned earth orbital missions directed toward accomplishing life science, astronomy, applications, and technology objectives.

Advanced Mission Studies

The objective of the advanced missions program is to examine advanced manned space-flight mission concepts and to develop technical information and cost data upon which future program decisions can be based.

SPACE APPLICATIONS

Outlays for space applications in 1971 are estimated to be 5.8 percent of the space outlays shown earlier. This program is designed to use the knowledge and resources gained from the space program for projects of economic benefit in more "earthbound" areas of national interest, such as geodesy, earth resources, communications, and weather forecasting. The following paragraphs include The Budget description of this area.

The objective of this activity is to achieve and expand the beneficial applications of space flights in the fields of meteorology, earth resources, geodesy, communication, and navigation. Specific objectives are to improve satellite instrumentation and data handling technology; to provide data for atmospheric, earth resources, and geodetic research; to participate in design and development of operational satellite systems as required; and to study advanced satellite systems.

The earth resources survey program continues to develop the technology for surveying the earth's resources from space. The major areas of interest are: agriculture/forestry, geology/mineralogy, hydrology/oceanography, and geography/cartography.

SPACE TECHNOLOGY

Advanced research and technology of use to future space flight is funded under this program area, which accounts for 11 percent of Space outlays in 1971. Work is done on spacecraft, launch vehicles, nuclear and other propulsion systems, and electronics.

This activity comprises R&D effort relating to space vehicle systems and operations and associated equipment and components for space missions. Emphasis is placed on space vehicle structures, auxiliary power systems, propulsion systems, and life support technology, with particular emphasis on their application to the development of a space shuttle and space station. The program includes continuation of development of a flight-type NERVA I nuclear rocket engine, having a thrust of about 75,000 pounds, to provide basic propulsion capability for future high-energy high-payload missions, including a reusable orbit-to-orbit transfer vehicle. The improvement of electronic systems for control, data acquisition, and communications continues.

SUPPORTING SPACE ACTIVITIES

Two program areas comprise supporting activities, which provide general support for the attainment of NASA mission objectives. This activity accounts for 14 percent of 1971 Space outlays. Its description, excerpted from The Budget, follows.

Tracking and Data Acquisition. Operation and equipment of stations of the NASA tracking and data acquisition networks are provided for here, as well as research and development to increase the capability of the specialized ground equipment.
Technology Utilization. The objective of this program is to accelerate the transfer of new advances in technology generated by NASA and NASA contractors into the economy.

NOTES

1. Executive Office of the President, Bureau of the Budget, The Budget in Brief, FY 1969 (Washington, D. C.: U. S. Government Printing Office, 1968), p. 31.

2. Public Law 85-568, 85th Cong., 2nd Sess., H. R. 12575, July, 1958, as quoted in NASA's First Semi-Annual Report to the Congress, 86th Cong., 1st Sess., 1959, pp. 50-51.

3. Ibid.

4. John F. Kennedy, State of the Union Message (Washington, D. C.: The White House, 1961).

5. Ibid.

6. Lyndon B. Johnson, Budget Message (Washington, D. C.: The White House, 1968).

7. Richard M. Nixon, Budget Message (Washington, D. C.: The White House, 1970).

CHAPTER **14** ENVIRONMENT

THE FIELD AS A WHOLE

The functional field of Environment includes programs designed to deal with the physical environment--air, land, and water--and man's impact upon it, especially, adverse effects. The Budget has no field specifically collecting such programs into a function. Because of the increasing attention that is being devoted to environmental problems and the likelihood of enlarged Government participation in alleviation of such problems, the programs that would seem to form the basis for such a functional field have been brought together here. The subfunctions included are water pollution (Federal Water Quality Administration), which The Budget includes in the field of Natural Resources; environmental control (Environmental Health Service of HEW and some of NIH) from the field of Health; and physical environment (Environmental Science Services Administration of Commerce) from The Budget field of Commerce and Transportation. Although other programs might be included in the Environment field, they are, generally, below the level of line items appearing in The Budget functional field breakout (e. g. , the AEC radiation protection program).

Although the environmental problems of which the nation is now so acutely aware have been building up for many years, it is only within the last few years that the public has realized the potential damage to its surroundings and health and been willing to support potential remedies with fiscal resources. This has been reflected in a spate of legislation at the Federal level in attempts to control various forms of pollution. There is differing opinion as to the matching of action to rhetoric, but there is general agreement that present levels of activity are inadequate to ameliorate the continuing deterioration of our environment.

Estimates have been made that the total cost to the country would be $20 billion a year for five years in order to handle

pollution adequately. It may be difficult to secure funds in
anywhere near these amounts for a problem that is largely
in the realm of a public rather than a private good. A second
difficulty in approaching environmental problems is the fact
that they stem largely from a highly industrialized and affluent
society. High individual rates of consumption of such things
as automobiles and electric power are a large part of the
pollution problem. Although technological advances may over-
come some negative aspects, such as the pollution from burn-
ing coal and oil for electric power and from the internal
combustion engine, there is some degree of trade-off between
economic growth, with its accompanying high levels of consumption, and the desire for a cleaner environment.

The costs of restoring and maintaining the quality of the
environment will be borne in many ways--partly in the costs
of products on the market, partly by governmental programs
at many levels. The National Environmental Policy Act of
1969 brings together many of the goals around which public
policy is coalescing. The purposes of the Act are

> To declare a national policy which will encourage
> productive and enjoyable harmony between man and
> his environment; to promote efforts which will pre-
> vent or eliminate damage to the environment and
> biosphere and stimulate the health and welfare of
> man; to enrich the understanding of the ecological
> systems and natural resources important to the
> Nation; and to establish a Council on Environmental
> Quality. [1]

Federal Government programs, the Act states, should be
conducted so that the Nation may--

> (1) fulfill the responsibilities of each generation as
> trustee of the environment for succeeding generations;
> (2) assure for all Americans safe, healthful,
> productive, and esthetically and culturally pleasing
> surroundings;
> (3) attain the widest range of beneficial uses of
> the environment without degradation, risk to health
> or safety, or other undesirable and unintended con-
> sequences;
> (4) preserve important historic, cultural, and
> natural aspects of our national heritage, and maintain,
> wherever possible, an environment which supports
> diversity and variety of individual choice;

(5) achieve a balance between population and
resource use which will permit high standards of
living and a wide sharing of life's amenities; and

(6) enhance the quality of renewable resources
and approach the maximum attainable recycling of
depletable resources. [2]

The goals of the Environment functional field contribute
to the supergoal of Public Welfare, discussed in Chapter 2.
They also contribute to the Economic Development supergoal
in its broader connotation, which includes social costs and
benefits.

Table 2 shows Federal outlays for Environment from 1961
to 1971 and the percent of total for each year. Because environmental concerns are a relatively recent function of the Federal
Government, outlays are low relative to other fields--never
as much as $1 billion and, for each year except 1971, only
0.2 percent or 0.3 percent of total Government outlays. Outlays for 1971 are expected to be 0.5 percent of all outlays.
Although it still ranks last, its relative growth over the decade
has been among the highest for the various fields.

From the standpoint of R&D, Environment is in a stronger
position relative to other fields--ranking eighth in both 1961
and 1971. This is only 1 percent of total R& D funds, however,
in 1971. In importance to its own field, R&D in Environment
was 13 percent of total field outlays in 1961 and increased to
17 percent in 1971. Although total outlays were increasing at
a high rate, R&D growth rates were even higher. More detailed discussion of the makeup of R&D in the Environment
field is contained in a later section.

A more detailed look at total outlays in this field appears
in Table 39, which shows the actual 1969, and estimated 1970
and 1971, outlays, as given in The Budget, broken down by
subfunction. The subfunctions shown here represent the
responsibilities of three departments prior to the proposed
establishment of an Environmental Protection Agency--
Interior, HEW, and Commerce, with Interior responsible for
somewhat more than 50 percent of the total and the remainder
split between HEW and Commerce.

Institutional responsibilities for these programs are likely
to undergo major change during the coming decade as some of
the programs are brought together. President Nixon has proposed a Government reorganization that would establish an
independent Environmental Protection Agency (EPA) and a
National Oceanic and Atmospheric Administration (NOAA) in

TABLE 39

Environment Outlay Details, FY's 1969-71
(In Millions of Dollars)

Program or Agency	Outlays		
	1969[a]	1970[b]	1971[b]
Water Pollution (Federal Water Quality Administration)	215	258	465
Environmental Control (Environmental Health Service--HEW)	132	164	189
Physical Environment (Environmental Science Services Administration--Commerce)	179	193	199
Total	526	615	853

[a]Actual.
[b]Estimate.

Source: Edited excerpts from The Budget, FY 1971, pp. 109, 116, and 151.

176

the Commerce Department. The proposed Environmental
Protection Administration brings together such programs as
the Federal Water Quality Administration from Interior and
the air pollution and solid waste management functions of HEW,
all included in the Environment field here. It would also include the pesticide programs of Agriculture and HEW and the
radiation protection function of AEC. The other subfunction
of the field presented here, physical environment, would be
the nucleus of a new administration within the Commerce Department, the Environmental Science Services Administration,
which would also include such programs as the fishery program
of Interior, the NSF Sea Grant program, and the Navy's
National Oceanographic Center.

WATER POLLUTION

This subfunction is made up of the Federal Water Quality
Administration in the Interior Department. The first Federal
water-pollution bill, passed in 1948, was administered by
the Public Health Service. It provided for grants to states to
plan, and loans to construct, sewage- and waste-treatment
works and for research by states and by the Federal Government. This 1948 Act was later amended to provide grants for
construction of plants. It was not until 1965 that the next
major amendments were made, creating a Federal Water
Pollution Control Administration (originally in Public Health
Service-HEW and later transferred to Interior) to administer
antipollution activities, to provide grants to states for demonstration projects, and to recommend (or set, in the absence
of state action) water-quality standards for interstate waters.
This administration is now called the Federal Water Quality
Administration. Recent legislative action included the Water
Quality Improvement Act of 1970, fixing responsibility for oil
spills on the owner or operator of a vessel or facility. It also
provided for acid mine drainage research; pollution control
of the Great Lakes; field laboratories land acquisition; clean
lakes research; and development of scientific knowledge on
the effects of pesticides on the environment.

ENVIRONMENTAL CONTROL

    The subfunction of environmental control encompasses the various programs of the Environmental Health Service in HEW and the National Institute for Environmental Health Sciences, a part of NIH (HEW). The Environmental Health Service deals with most pollution problems aside from water pollution--air pollution, solid waste disposal, and radiological and occupational health. States are being assisted in establishing air quality standards and enforcement plans. Research expenditures are rising for control of sulfur oxides, nitrogen oxides, and motor vehicle emissions. The National Institute for Environmental Health Sciences supports research on the health aspects of environmental pollutants.

    The Federal Government became involved in the air pollution problem, in 1955, with the passage of the Air Pollution Control Act, which authorized the Public Health Service to conduct air pollution research. A broader law was passed in 1963--the Clean Air Act of 1963. An amendment to this Act, in 1965, directed the Secretary of HEW to establish emission standards for new motor vehicles and authorized accelerated research on pollution caused by sulfur oxides. In 1966, grants were authorized to state, local, and regional agencies for maintaining air pollution control programs. The most far-reaching air pollution control bill enacted was the Air Quality Act of 1967. It authorized the Secretary of HEW to designate air-quality control regions throughout the nation; provided full Federal financing for regional control commissions to be established by state governors; and empowered the HEW Secretary to enforce air-quality standards in the control regions if the states failed to adopt such standards and an acceptable pollution abatement plan within fifteen months after receiving HEW's guidelines on air purity. The Act also authorized the Secretary to go to court to enforce any violations of standards in an air-quality region after 180 days' notice of violation. The Act authorized expenditures for research on pollution caused by fuel combustion and required registration of all fuel additives with the HEW Secretary.

    The first Federal legislation dealing with solid waste was the Solid Waste Disposal Act of 1965, which was an amendment to the Clean Air Act. The purpose of the Act was to begin a national R&D program for new improved methods of solid waste disposal and to provide technical and financial aid to state and local governments in developing, establishing, and conducting solid waste disposal programs.

PHYSICAL ENVIRONMENT

The subfunction on the physical environment is the title given to the activities of the Environmental Science Services Administration in the Department of Commerce. A reorganization plan in 1965 combined the Weather Bureau, the Coast and Geodetic Survey, and the Radio Propagation Laboratory into the present Environmental Science Services Administration. This Administration seeks to improve understanding of the atmosphere, the oceans, and the earth in order to provide weather forecasts and warnings, flood warnings, earth and marine descriptions and maps, and information on atmospheric conditions that affect man or materials in space. R&D is of considerable and growing importance to this agency, including the R&D of improved weather satellites.

This subfunction differs from the others included in the Environment field in that it does not deal primarily with pollution and degradation of the environment but with a general understanding of natural aspects of our environment. This agency is expected to be the nucleus of a New Oceanic and Atmospheric Administration (NOAA) in the Commerce Department. The Federal interest in oceanography has increased substantially in the past decade, with the realization of the new strategic importance and economic value of the oceans. Although this agency has a major interest in this field, the largest expenditures are, actually, in connection with National Security--especially antisubmarine warfare--and appear under that field. These outlays would, for the most part, remain with DOD rather than being transferred to the proposed NOAA.

RESEARCH AND DEVELOPMENT

In 1971, R&D for Environment is about 1 percent of total Government R&D funds. But it is about 17 percent of total outlays in the Environment field. Table 40 shows the R&D expenditures for 1969-71 for the three agencies discussed.

TABLE 40

Environment R&D Conduct Expenditures by Program Area,
FY's 1969-71
(In Millions of Dollars)

Program Area	Agency	1969[a]	1970[b]	1971[b]
Environmental Health Services and National Institute of Environmental Health Sciences	HEW	64.9	72.5	82.2
Environmental Science Services Administration	Commerce	26.1	27.7	29.4
Federal Water Quality Administration	Interior	24.7	31.0	33.5
Total		115.7	131.2	145.2

[a] Actual.
[b] Estimate.

Source: Data obtained from the Department of Health, Education, and Welfare; the Department of Commerce; and the Department of the Interior.

Environmental Health Service and National Institute
for Environmental Health Sciences (HEW)*

The environmental Health Service awards grants to conduct research into air pollution problems. Contracts relating
to fuels and vehicles are used to accelerate R&D into new and
improved methods, having industrywide application, for the
prevention and control of air pollution resulting from the combustion of fuels. The solid waste program is designed to ensure
proper health protection and improved solid wastes disposal
practices and technology through research, training, demonstration, development, and systems planning.

Other research is funded for the prevention and control of
occupational hazards and diseases; the sources, levels, and
effects of radiation; and safeguarding the sanitary quality of
water supplies.

Environmental Science Services Administration
(Department of Commerce)

This agency includes the U.S. Weather Bureau, the Coast
and Geodetic Survey, and the Central Radio Propagation Laboratory in Boulder, Colorado. This activity consists of meteoro-
logical R&D designed to improve the weather forecasting and
warning services of the Environmental Science Services Administration by gaining a fuller understanding of the composition, dynamics, and circulation of the atmosphere and developing
better instrumentation and techniques for weather observing and
forecasting.

River and flood forecasts and warnings include R&D for
further improvements in the river and flood forecasting services
and development of specialized equipment related to forecasts
and water resources services.

Earth description, mapping, and charting include research
directed toward understanding the intricate processes and
phenomena of the solid earth, such as seismological studies
and warnings, determining the size and shape of the earth, and
improvement in the aeronautical charting program.

---

*Descriptions of the R&D program areas are excerpted
from The Budget.

Federal Water Quality Administration
(Department of the Interior)

This Administration in the Department of the Interior finances research and field investigations and studies of an applied nature. The purpose is to test and illustrate the applicability of research findings and newly developed techniques to problems of water pollution, particularly those related to industrial waste pollution problems: combined sewer problems, advanced waste treatment, water purification, and joint treatment of municipal and industrial wastes problems. Other expenditures are made to carry out activities in the Federal Water Quality Administration laboratories, to conduct field studies and demonstrations, and to provide technical management for the grants and contract programs.

NOTES

1. Public Law 91-190, 91st Cong., 2nd Sess., S. 1075, January 1, 1970, 83 Stat. 852.

2. Ibid.

CHAPTER **15** THE LIKELY FUTURE

SUMMARY: ALL FUNCTIONAL FIELDS

Looking into the future is always hazardous and judgmental (even though based primarily on past data trends, as in this study), and knowledgeable people do have honest differences of opinion. For this reason, such judgments are made explicit in this study and put in a format that will enable others to utilize their best judgment. The likely relative growth indicators used are based upon past trends in funding levels and, in a few instances, judgments about the possibility of breaks in these trends due to already apparent changes in priorities that are discussed in the text. Some unexpected changes in priorities and the initiation of new fields and programs will, undoubtedly, occur during the next decade, as they have in the past, but the nature of these is not predictable.

The relative growth concept (used in this study to describe the immediate past and likely future) is a comparison of the 1969-71 change in expenditures for each functional field and its subfunctions with the change in total Federal Government funding between 1969 and 1971. The immediate past and present is believed to provide the best indicator of probable trends in the near future. As a result, the likely future growth indicators for the functional fields and their subfunctions are primarily based upon their growth relative to the total Government in the immediate past.

It is important to make explicit that this study does not forecast the likely future of total Government outlays or total Federal R&D funding. What the indicators do present is the relative likely future of the individual functional fields and their subfunctions based upon past trends. In other words, a likely future indicator of "above average" for a field or subfunction indicates that its funding is expected to grow at a higher rate than that of the Government as a whole, whatever that rate may be.

Since total Government outlays grew by 8 percent between

1969 and 1971, the growth of outlays in a functional field or subfunction of 6 percent to 10 percent is described as average, and a growth of over 15 percent as well above average. Since total Government funding of R&D conduct declined by 4 percent between 1969 and 1971, any increase for a functional field or subfunction's R&D conduct expenditures is considered above average, and an increase of over 5 percent is considered well above average.

Table 42 summarizes an estimate of the likely future relative growth for each of the functional fields in terms of total outlays (left side of table) and R&D conduct expenditures (right side of table). 1971 outlays and percent of total field are shown to indicate the absolute dollars and relative importance of each of the fields.

The relative growth concept is a comparison of the percent change between 1969 and 1971 in expenditures for each field with the total Federal Government percent change. These figures are shown in the third column on each side of Table 42, and the fourth column shows the results of this comparison on the basis of the scale shown in Table 41.

The final column on each side of Table 42 shows a forecast of the likely future in relative growth terms. Where the information reviewed and studied to prepare this book provides no indication of a break with the immediate past and present (i.e., no reason to expect an increase or decrease in priority), this column has the same term as the preceding column for 1969 to 1971. Where there is some basis for expecting a change in priority, the terms in this column will differ from the preceding column, and the discussion preceding the table will reflect the rationale. The sections that follow, on the individual functional fields, discuss the likely future of each in greater detail and analyze the subfunctions in each field based upon the scale shown above.

Looking at the likely future in terms of total outlays (left side of Table 42), the following fields have experienced well above average growth in the immediate past, and this is expected to continue: Income Security and Welfare; Health; Education, Knowledge, and Manpower; General Government; Housing and Community Development; and Environment. Commerce, Transportation, and Communications is expected to continue its above-average relative growth and Natural Resources is expected to continue at below-average relative growth rates. The following fields are likely to continue the well below average growth rates of the immediate past: National Security; Agriculture and Rural Development; International Relations; and Space.

TABLE 41

Relative Growth Comparison Scale

Total Outlays		Total R&D Conduct Expenditures	
Percent Change, 1969-71	Growth Relative to Average, 1969-71	Percent Change, 1969-71	Growth Relative to Average, 1969-71
Total Federal Government			
+ 8	Average	- 4	Average
Functional Fields			
> +15	Well above	> + 5	Well above
+11 to +15	Above	+ 1 to +5	Above
+ 6 to +10	About average	- 6 to 0	About average
0 to + 5	Below	-10 to -7	Below
< 0	Well below	< -10	Well below

Source: Federal Government data from The Budget, FY 1971.

TABLE 42

All Functional Fields--Immediate Past and
Likely Future Relative Growth
(In Millions of Dollars)

Functional Field	Total Outlays			Growth Relative to Average	
	Dollars, 1971	Percent of Total	Percent Change, 1969-71	1969-71	Likely Future
National Security	72,377	39	-10	Well Below	Well Below
Income Security and Welfare	56,173	30	+32	Well Above	Well Above
Health	16,652	9	+26	Well Above	Well Above
Education, Knowledge, and Manpower	10,060	5	+22	Well Above	Well Above
Commerce, Transportation, and Communications	8,770	5	+12	Above Average	Above Average
Agriculture and Rural Development	5,364	3	-14	Well Below	Well Below
General Government	4,084	2	+42	Well Above	Well Above
International Relations	3,589	2	-5	Well Below	Well Below
Housing and Community Development	3,466	2	+68	Well Above	Well Above
Natural Resources	2,882	1.5	+4	Below	Below
Space	2,765	1.5	-24	Well Below	Well Below
Environment	853	0.5	+62	Well Above	Well Above
Total	187,035	100	+8		

186

Functional Field	Total R&D Conduct Expenditures			Growth Relative to Average	
	Dollars, 1971	Percent of Total	Percent Change, 1969-71	1969-71	Likely Future
National Security	8,113	54	-1	About Average	About Average
Income Security and Welfare	49	0.3	+21	Well Above	Well Above
Health	1,241	8	+11	Well Above	Well Above
Education, Knowledge, and Manpower	1,211	8	+5	Above Average	Above Average
Commerce, Transportation, and Communications	425	3	+32	Well Above	Well Above
Agriculture and Rural Development	259	2	+10	Well Above	Well Above
General Government	17	0.1	+188	Well Above	Well Above
International Relations	28	0.2	+85	Well Above	Well Above
Housing and Community Development	73	0.5	+77	Well Above	Well Above
Natural Resources	714	5	+5	Above Average	Above Average
Space	2,709	18	-24	Well Below	Well Below
Environment	145	1	+25	Well Above	Well Above
Total	14,982	100	-4		

Source: Basic data from The Budget, FY 1971.

Turning to the likely future in terms of R&D expenditures (right side of Table 42), the expectation that a well below average relative growth rate will continue for Space, the second largest R&D field, and an average relative R&D growth rate for National Security, the largest R&D field, allows all other fields to continue well above average or above-average relative growth rates as follows:

Well Above Average

Health

Commerce, Transportation, and
  Communications

Agriculture and Rural Development

Environment

Housing and Community Development

Income Security and Welfare

International Relations

General Government

Above Average

Education, Knowledge, and Manpower

Natural Resources

Several points should be considered in evaluating these forecasts. First, and most important, is the fact that the various fields are at very different funding levels, as 1971 dollar and percent of total columns on Table 42 indicate. Therefore, a lower relative growth rate for a large field can mean as much or even more in terms of incremental funding than a higher relative growth rate for a smaller field.

Secondly, as pointed out in Chapter 2, the portion of total outlays spent on R&D has been going down, especially in the last few years, when total Federal R&D expenditures have been going down and total outlays have been going up. This presents the possibility of negative future growth rates, as was the case for total R&D between 1969 and 1971. If such a possibility occurs, an above-average growth rate could be very low or even negative.

Finally, it should be noted that all discussion of past or future growth rates is in actual, rather than real, dollar terms. This means that figures have not been discounted for inflation, and real increases in effort will be smaller than actual dollar increases by the rate of increase in costs. [1]

NATIONAL SECURITY

The technique used in the other functional fields regarding
the likely future is not applicable to this field, because in
National Security, the United States, to a large extent, is re-
acting to threats (real or potential), which are external in
nature. In addition, a large part of the information required,
even to speculate about future expenditure trends for individual
National Security subfunctions or programs, is classified and
not generally available. Nonetheless, a few general comments
about likely total expenditures for National Security can be
made, although dealing with detailed subfunctions and programs
is beyond the scope of this study.
1.   Relative to other functional fields, changes in National
Security are likely to be well below average, especially in the
post-Vietnam period, and National Security is expected to
continue to decline as a percent of total outlays. There is a
very real possibility that it will fall during the decade from its
number one rank, as Income Security and Welfare outlays increase at a faster rate than National Security outlays.
2.   There is much discussion about how much of the direct
costs of the Vietnam War will continue to be expended for
National Security functions in the post-Vietnam period. It is
likely that a significant portion will continue to be expended for
this field but that some will also be released for other purposes.
It is for this reason that changes in funding dollars for National
Security are expected to be well below average growth rates.
3.   In terms of R&D, the National Security functional field is
likely to continue to rank first, and it is probable that the relative decline in percent of total experienced during 1961-66,
which was reversed in the 1966-71 period, will stabilize at
about half the R&D budget. This would mean a continuation of
the about-average growth rates of the past few years rather
than a recurrence of the below-average growth rates experienced in the pre-Vietnam War period.

INCOME SECURITY AND WELFARE

Table 43 provides an estimate of the likely future relative
growth for each of the field's subfunctions in terms of total
outlays (left side of table), and R&D conduct expenditures (right
side of table). Outlays and percent of total field for 1971 are

TABLE 43

Income Security and Welfare--Immediate Past
and Likely Future Relative Growth
(In Millions of Dollars)

Subfunction	Total Outlays			Growth Relative To Average		Total R&D Conduct Expenditures			Growth Relative To Average	
	Dollars, 1971	Percent of Total	Percent Change, 1969-71	1969-71	Likely Future	Dollars, 1971	Percent of Total	Percent Change, 1969-71	1969-71	Likely Future
Retirement and Social Insurance	41,895	75	+30	Well Above	Well Above					
Public Assistance	7,035	13	+65	Well Above	Well Above					
Social and Individual Services	1,454	3	+64	Well Above	Well Above	49	100	+21	Well Above	Well Above
Veterans Income Security	5,789	10	+10	About Average	About Average					
Total	56,173	100	+32	Well Above	Well Above	49	100	+21	Well Above	Well Above
Total Federal Government			+ 8					- 4		

Source: Basic data from The Budget, FY 1971, and individual agencies.

shown to indicate the absolute dollar and relative importance
to the field for each of the subfunctions.

The following points summarize the likely future for the
field and its subfunctions:
1.   It is likely that total expenditures for the Income Security
and Welfare functional field will continue to grow at well above
the average growth rate for all functional fields.   The field
may surpass National Security in expenditures by the end of
the decade.
2.   Priorities within the field are fairly consistent, with all
subfunctions likely to continue to grow at well above average
rates, except for veterans income security, which is likely to
continue at about the average growth rate.
3.   While R&D is likely to grow at well above average rates,
its importance to the field is likely to continue to be minor
(well under 1 percent of all outlays in 1961 and 1971) and remain under 1 percent of total Government R&D.

HEALTH

Table 44 provides an estimate of the likely future relative
growth for each of the subfunctions of the Health field.   The
following points summarize the likely future for the field and
its subfunctions:
1.   There is every reason to expect the Health functional field
to continue growing at well above average rates.   Relative increases in the recent past have been extraordinary--from 2
percent to 9 percent of total Government outlays and from a
rank of eight in 1961 to a rank of three (out of twelve) in 1971.
This functional field is one of the fastest growing, and there
is no reason to doubt its continued rapid growth in the near
future.
2.   The above applies to both Health outlays and Health R&D,
with the exception of the subfunction of veterans hospital and
medical care, which is above average, rather than well above
average in growth of total outlays.   In R&D, the AEC biology
and medicine program is likely to grow at about average rates.
3.   Medicare and Medicaid and other financing of medical
services is about four-fifths of total outlays in this functional
field, and all indications point to even larger future increases
in expenditures.

TABLE 44

Health--Immediate Past and Likely Future Relative Growth
(In Millions of Dollars)

Subfunction	Total Outlays			Growth Relative To Average		Total R&D Conduct Expenditures			Growth Relative To Average	
	Dollars, 1971	Percent of Total	Percent Change, 1969-71	1969-71	Likely Future	Dollars, 1971	Percent of Total	Percent Change, 1969-71	1969-71	Likely Future
Development of Health Resources	2,303	14	+16	Well Above	Well Above	HEW: 1,906	88	+12	Well Above	Well Above
Providing or Financing Medical Services	12,106	73	+30	Well Above	Well Above					
Prevention and Control of Health Problems	449	3	+28	Well Above	Well Above	AEC: 86	7	0	About Average	About Average
Veterans Hospital and Medical	1,796	11	+15	Above	Above	58	5	+18	Well Above	Well Above
Total	16,652	100	+26	Well Above	Well Above	1,241	100	+11	Well Above	Well Above
Total Federal Government			+ 8					- 4		

Source: Basic data from The Budget, FY 1971, and individual agencies.

EDUCATION, KNOWLEDGE, AND MANPOWER

Table 45 provides an estimate of the likely future relative growth for each of the subfunctions of the Education, Knowledge, and Manpower field. The following points summarize the likely future for the field and its subfunctions:

1.   There is little reason to doubt that past trends will continue and result in well above average increases in funding for the Education, Knowledge, and Manpower functional field (especially, post-Vietnam). Increased priority for this field is likely to make it one of the fastest growing fields of Federal activity.

2.   If the functional field is considered in terms of its major component parts, there is good reason to expect the Education and Manpower portions to grow rapidly and the Knowledge portion (NSF, AEC, and NASA) to grow slowly. Although NSF's immediate past growth was below average, the likely future growth is expected to be above average as a result of recent changes in legislation, which broadened NSF's authority, and as a result of greater support for research that previously had been supported by DOD.

3.   In terms of R&D interest, this functional field is likely to continue to be more R&D-oriented than most (R&D accounting for 12 percent of all expenditures in 1971). However, larger growth is likely to come in education activities other than R&D.

COMMERCE, TRANSPORTATION, AND COMMUNICATIONS

Table 46 provides an estimate of the likely future relative growth for each of the subfunctions of the Commerce, Transportation, and Communications field. The following points summarize the likely future for the field and its subfunctions:

1.   Although the likely future of the field of Commerce, Transportation, and Communications is more uncertain than most fields, because priority decisions are still to be made regarding the highway construction and mass transit programs, there is little chance that it will rise from its present rank of five (out of twelve), although it is probable that its present 5 percent of total outlays will increase somewhat.

2.   However, within this heterogeneous field, the subfunctions

TABLE 45

Education, Knowledge, and Manpower--Immediate Past and Likely Future Relative Growth
(In Millions of Dollars)

Subfunction	Total Outlays Dollars, 1971	Percent of Total	Percent Change, 1969-71	Growth Relative to Average 1969-71	Likely Future	Total R&D Conduct Expenditures Dollars, 1971	Percent of Total	Percent Change, 1969-71	Growth Relative to Average 1969-71	Likely Future
Elementary and Secondary Education	2,710	27	+ 9	About Average	Above	a	a	a	a	a
Higher Education	1,449	14	+18	Well Above	Well Above	a	a	a	a	a
Vocational Education	329	3	+26	Well Above	Well Above	a	a	a	a	a
Science Education and Basic Research	1,215	12	<- 1			1,039	86	+ 3	About Average	About Average
National Aeronautics and Space Administration	(451)	(5)	(-1)	Well Below	Well Below	(446)	(37)	(-1)	Well Above	Well Above
National Science Foundation	(490)	(5)	(0)	Below	Above	(319)	(26)	(+14)	Well Above	Well Above
Atomic Energy Commission Physical Research	(274)	(3)	(- 1)	Well Below	Well Below	(274)	(23)	(0)	About Average	About Average
Veterans Education, Training, and Rehabilitation	1,206	12	+72	Well Above	Well Above	---	---	---	---	---
Other Education Aids	411	4	+10	About Average	About Average	115	9	+11	Well Above	Well Above
Manpower Training	1,720	17	+44	Well Above	Well Above	50	4	+22	Well Above	Well Above
Other Manpower Aids	1,034	10	+28	Well Above	Well Above	7	1	+ 5	Above	Above
Subtotal	10,074	100				1,211	100	+ 5	Above	Above
Adjustments	-14									
Total	10,060		+22	Well Above	Well Above			- 4		
Total Federal Government			+ 8							

aAll Office of Education R&D is included under "Other Aids to Education" subfunction.

Source: Basic data from The Budget, FY 1971, and individual agencies.

TABLE 46

Commerce, Transportation, and Communications--Immediate Past and Likely Future Relative Growth
(In Millions of Dollars)

Subfunction	Total Outlays			Growth Relative to Average		Total R&D Conduct Expenditures			Growth Relative to Average	
	Dollars, 1971	Percent of Total	Percent Change, 1969-71	1969-71	Likely Future	Dollars, 1971	Percent of Total	Percent Change, 1969-71	1969-71	Likely Future
Air Transportation	1,852	20	+53	Well Above	Well Above	236	56	+15	Well Above	Well Above
Water Transportation	938	10	+9	About Average	About Average	26	6	+79	Well Above	Well Above
Ground Transportation	4,881	52	+11	Above	Well Above	68	16	+82	Well Above	Well Above
Postal Service	382	4	-58	Well Below	Above	41	10	+98	Well Above	Well Above
Advancement of Business (Other Commerce R&D)	461	5	+97	Well Above	Well Above	40	9	+5	Above	Above
Area and Regional Development	710	8	+22	Well Above	Well Above	a	a	a	a	a
Regulation of Business	124	1	+16	Well Above	Well Above	1	<1			
Other Transportation R&D	---	--	--	--	--	13	3	+124	Well Above	Well Above
Total, Less FDIC	9,346	100								
FDIC[b]	-359									
Subtotal	8,987									
Adjustments	-217									
Total	8,770	--	+12	Above	Above	425	100	+32	Well Above	Well Above
Total Federal Government			+8					-4		

[a] Included in Advancement of Business.
[b] Because Federal Deposit Insurance Corporation was such a large negative expenditure, it was excluded from total expenditures for purposes of assessing the likely future.

Note: Figures may not add to totals because of rounding.

Source: Basic data from The Budget, FY 1971, and individual agencies.

of ground transportation, air transportation, and area and regional development show promise of well above average growth rates in total outlays. While the immediate past growth rate for ground transportation outlays is above average, the likely future growth is expected to be well above average as a result of an increased priority on mass transportation, as expressed in recent pronouncements by the Administration and enactments by the Congress.

3.   The well below average immediate past growth rate for postal service outlays is expected to increase to above average as the effects of wage increases for postal workers takes hold. However, proposed postal reform measures and transferring postal services to a public corporation structure could result in a system whereby Federal subsidy of postal services disappears entirely as users fully pay for future cost increases.

4.   In terms of R&D interest, this functional field is less R&D-oriented than average, devoting 4.8 percent of total outlays in 1971 to R&D. But, this is up considerably from the 2.4 percent in 1961, and, although less than 3 percent of total Government R&D, all subfunctions have well above average likely future growth in R&D expenditures. Continued and increased interest in advanced communications technology (including satellite communications) and advanced transportation technology (including aircraft, highway safety, traffic control, urban transit, navigation, and high-speed ground transportation) is likely.

AGRICULTURE AND RURAL DEVELOPMENT

Table 47 provides an estimate of the likely future relative growth for each of the subfunctions of the Agriculture and Rural Development field. The following points summarize the likely future for the field and its subfunctions:

1.   Agriculture and Rural Development dollar allocations vary much more than most of the other functional fields because the farm income stabilization subfunction accounts for about 80 percent of the total and is dependent upon the level of crop yields for supported commodities in any given year. Nonetheless, it is likely that future relative growth in total expenditures will continue to be well below average, although this field will remain approximately in the middle of all functional fields.

2.   Within the total functional field, the farm income stabilization subfunction is likely to continue at well below average

TABLE 47

Agriculture and Rural Development--Immediate Past and Likely Future Relative Growth
(In Millions of Dollars)

Subfunction	Total Outlays			Growth Relative to Average		Total R&D Conduct Expenditures			Growth Relative to Average	
	Dollars, 1971	Percent of Total	Percent Change, 1969-71	1969-71	Likely Future	Dollars, 1971	Percent of Total	Percent Change, 1969-71	1969-71	Likely Future
Farm Income Stabilization	4,467	83	-11	Well Below	Well Below					
Rural Housing and Public Facilities	-176	-3	a	a	a					
Agricultural Land and Water Resource	317	6	- 8	Well Below	Well Below					
Research and Other Agricultural Services	799	15	+24	Well Above	Well Above	259	100	+10	Well Above	Well Above
Subtotal	5,405									
Adjustments	-41									
Total	5,364	100	-14	Well Below	Well Below	259	100.0	±10	Well Above	Well Above
Total Federal Government			+ 8					- 4		

aIncludes significant amount of lending and repayment and sales of loans; therefore, it is highly variable and unpredictable.

Note: Figures may not add to totals because of rounding.

Source: Basic data from The Budget, FY 1971, and individual agencies.

relative growth; agricultural land and water resources, well
below average; and research and other agricultural services,
well above average.

3.   R&D expenditures are likely to continue at well above
average relative growth.

GENERAL GOVERNMENT

Table 48 provides an estimate of the likely future relative
growth for each of the subfunctions of the General Government
field.   The following points summarize the likely future for
the field and its subfunctions:

1.   Growth in expenditures for the General Government functional field is likely to continue well above average.

2.   Eight of the nine subfunctions are expected to continue
well above average growth and the ninth (general property and
records management) is expected to continue above-average
growth.

3.   R&D in this functional field is very small, but almost entirely in relation to the law enforcement and justice subfunction
and, therefore, can be expected to continue to increase at
well above average growth rates.

INTERNATIONAL RELATIONS

Table 49 provides an estimate of the likely future relative
growth for each of the subfunctions of the International Relations field.   The following points summarize the likely future
for the field and its subfunctions:

1.   It is likely that relative growth in expenditures for the
International Relations functional field will continue to be well
below average and that the field will slip further in rank from
the eighth place in 1971.

2.   All subfunctions are likely to experience less-than-average
relative growth, except for the conduct of foreign affairs,
which is likely to maintain above-average growth in expenditures.

3.   R&D expenditures are likely to continue well above average
relative growth rates but are only 0.8 percent of total expenditures in this field.   Technical assistance funding is not included
in R&D and amounts to more than 5 percent of the field's total
outlays.

TABLE 48

General Government--Immediate Past and Likely Future Relative Growth
(In Millions of Dollars)

Subfunction	Total Outlays					Total R&D Conduct Expenditures				
	Dollars, 1971	Percent of Total	Percent Change, 1969-71	Growth Relative to Average 1969-71	Growth Relative to Average Likely Future	Dollars, 1971	Percent of Total	Percent Change, 1969-71	Growth Relative to Average 1969-71	Growth Relative to Average Likely Future
Legislative Functions	242	6	+26	Well Above	Well Above					
Judicial Functions	135	3	+23	Well Above	Well Above					
Executive Direction and Management	45	1	+45	Well Above	Well Above					
Central Fiscal Operations	1,345	31	+23	Well Above	Well Above	1	4	+17	Well Above	Well Above
General Property and Records Management	632	15	+11	Above	Above					
Central Personnel Management	184	4	+26	Well Above	Well Above					
Law Enforcement and Justice	1,027	24	+92	Well Above	Well Above	17	96	+207	Well Above	Well Above
National Capital Region	414	10	+156	Well Above	Well Above					
Other General Government	315	7	+18	Well Above	Well Above					
Subtotal	4,339	100								
Adjustments	-255									
Total Outlays	4,084	100	+42	Well Above	Well Above	17	100	+188	Well Above	Well Above
Total Federal Government			+ 8					- 4		

Note: Figures may not add to totals because of rounding.

Source: Basic data from The Budget, FY 1971, and individual agencies.

199

TABLE 49

International Relations--Immediate Past and Likely Future Relative Growth
(In Millions of Dollars)

Subfunction	Total Outlays			Growth Relative to Average		Total R&D Conduct Expenditures			Growth Relative to Average	
	Dollars, 1971	Percent of Total	Percent Change, 1969-71	1969-71	Likely Future	Dollars, 1971	Percent of Total	Percent Change, 1969-71	1969-71	Likely Future
Economic and Financial Assistance	2,357	61	- 3	Well Below	Well Below	23	84	+147	Well Above	Well Above
Food for Peace	852	22	-13	Well Below	Well Below	---	---	---	---	---
Foreign Information and Exchange Activities	241	6	+ 2	Below	Below	<1	1	+50	Well Above	Well Above
Conduct of Foreign Affairs	412	11	+11	Above	Above	4	15	-22	Well Below	Well Below
Subtotal	3,862									
Adjustments	-273									
Total	3,589	100	- 5	Well Below	Well Below	28	100	+85	Well Above	Well Above
Total Federal Government			+ 8					- 4		

Source: Basic data from The Budget, FY 1971, and individual agencies.

HOUSING AND COMMUNITY DEVELOPMENT

Table 50 provides an estimate of the likely future relative growth for each of the subfunctions of the Housing and Community Development field. The following points summarize the likely future for the field and its subfunctions:

1.   It is likely that expenditures for the Housing and Community Development functional field will continue to grow at well above average rates and that the field will rise in rank from nine (out of twelve) in 1971.

2.   Expenditures for all subfunctions in this field are likely to continue to grow at well above average rates. Although net lending has been declining recently, expenditures doubled in the 1969-71 period.

3.   Growth in R&D associated with this field is also likely to continue at well above average rates, as attempts are made to encourage new ways of building and as OEO focuses more on evaluation and experimentation. R&D is still, however, a very small part of the total field.

NATURAL RESOURCES

Table 51 provides an estimate of the likely future relative growth for each of the subfunctions of the Natural Resources field. The following points summarize the likely future for the field and its subfunctions:

1.   There is little chance that the Natural Resources field will rise to its 1961 rank of six from its present rank of ten (out of twelve fields). Modest increases in funding dollars are likely to continue but, relative to other functional fields, they are likely to be below-average percent increases.

2.   However, if the functional field is considered in terms of its gross outlays by subfunction before deduction of receipts from the public, there is good reason to expect most subfunctions to show above-average increases. The nuclear energy portion will continue to decrease in importance and show well below average increases.

3.   In terms of R&D interest, this functional field is likely to continue to be more R&D-oriented than most and grow at above-average rates. R&D in some of the smaller subfunctions is likely to grow at well above average rates, but the major R&D subfunction of nuclear energy is expected to grow at about-average rates.

TABLE 50

Housing and Community Development--Immediate Past and Likely Future Relative Growth
(In Millions of Dollars)

Subfunction	Total Expenditures^a			Growth Relative to Average		Total R&D Conduct Expenditures			Growth Relative to Average	
	Dollars, 1971	Percent of Total	Percent Change, 1969-71	1969-71	Likely Future	Dollars, 1971	Percent of Total	Percent Change, 1969-71	1969-71	Likely Future
Low- and Moderate-Income Housing Aids	861	24	+150	Well Above	Well Above					
Community Planning and Administration	97	3	+106	Well Above	Well Above	36	49	+31	Well Above	Well Above
Community Environment	1,127	32	+ 89	Well Above	Well Above					
Community Facilities	202	6	+ 98	Well Above	Well Above					
Concentrated Community Development	1,244	35	+ 81	Well Above	Well Above	37	51	+177	Well Above	Well Above
Subtotal	3,532	100				73	100			
Maintenance of Housing Mortgage Market	-362									
Total Expenditures	3,170									
Net Lending	-297									
Total Outlays	3,466		+ 68	Well Above	Well Above			+77	Well Above	Well Above
Total Federal Government			+ 8					- 4		

^aSee Table 30 and the accompanying explanation for use of expenditures rather than total outlays.
Note: Figures may not add up to totals because of rounding.

Source: Basic data from The Budget, FY 1971, and individual agencies.

TABLE 51

Natural Resources--Immediate Past and Likely Future Relative Growth
(In Millions of Dollars)

Subfunction	Total Outlays			Growth Relative to Average		Total R&D Conduct Expenditures			Growth Relative to Average	
	Dollars, 1971	Percent of Total	Percent Change, 1969-71	1969-71	Likely Future	Dollars, 1971	Percent of Total	Percent Change, 1969-71	1969-71	Likely Future
Water Resources and Power	2,475	50	+21	Well Above	Well Above	54	8	+ 2	Above	Above
Nuclear Energy	844	17	- 2	Well Below	Well Below	443	62	- 3	About Average	About Average
Land Management	771	16	+20	Well Above	Well Above	52	7	+19	Well Above	Well Above
Mineral Resources	110	2	+55	Well Above	Well Above	67	9	+54	Well Above	Well Above
Recreational Resources	546	11	+47	Well Above	Well Above	21	3	+17	Well Above	Well Above
Other Natural Resources Programs	183	4	+14	Above	Above	77	11	+13	Well Above	Well Above
Subtotal	4,930	100				714	100			
Receipts from the Public	-2,048									
Total Outlays	2,882		+ 4	Below	Below			+ 5	Above	Above
Total Federal Government			+ 8					- 4		

Note: Figures may not add up to totals because of rounding.

Source: Basic data from The Budget, FY 1971, and individual agencies.

SPACE

Table 52 provides an estimate of the likely future relative
growth for each of the subfunctions of the Space field.   The
following points summarize the likely future for the field and
its subfunctions:
1.   The data in both this chapter and in Chapter 2 indicate
that there is little likelihood that the Space field will recapture
its middecade rank of five (out of twelve).   Space has suffered
a significant decline in funding dollars in recent years.   The
data indicate that Space is likely to continue to show well below
average relative growth.
2.   Only the Space Applications subfunction within this field
has been able to grow, with manned space-flight, space technology, and supporting space activities subfunctions showing
well below average growth in the immediate past.   These
trends are expected to continue.
3.   Since virtually all Space expenditures are classed as R&D,
there is no difference in total expenditure and R&D expenditure trends.   However, it is important to note that, despite
declines in absolute dollar funding, the Space field is still
second to National Security in R&D expenditures and more
R&D-oriented than any other field.

ENVIRONMENT

Table 53 provides an estimate of the likely future relative
growth for each of the subfunctions of the Environment field.
The following points summarize the likely future for the field
and its subfunctions:
1.   The Environment field is expected to grow at well above
average rates during the next decade.   This is to be expected
of a field that has just begun to emerge as a major area of
Government concern.   Although its outlays are well below
the fields just above it in rank, it may rise in rank by the end
of the decade, from twelve to a rank of eleven or ten.
2.   Within the field, the two subfunctions dealing primarily
with pollution problems are expected to grow at the highest
rates, but the physical environment subfunction Environmental
Science Services Administration will grow at rates higher than
average for the whole Government.
3.   In terms of R&D interest, all subfunctions are expected

TABLE 52

Space--Immediate Past and Likely Future Relative Growth
(In Millions of Dollars)

Subfunction	Total Outlays			Growth Relative To Average		Total R&D Conduct Expenditures			Growth Relative to Average	
	Dollars, 1971	Percent of Total	Percent Change, 1969-71	1969-71	Likely Future	Dollars, 1971	Percent of Total	Percent Change, 1969-71	1969-71	Likely Future
Manned Space-Flight	1,937	70	-30	Well Below	Well Below	1,917	71	-30	Well Below	Well Below
Space Applications	161	6	+42	Well Above	Well Above	161	6	+43	Well Above	Well Above
Space Technology	306	11	-11	Well Below	Well Below	297	11	-10	Well Below	Well Below
Supporting Space Activities	376	13	- 4	Well Below	Well Below	335	12	-10	Well Below	Well Below
Subtotal	2,780									
Adjustments	- 15									
Total	2,765	100	-24	Well Below	Well Below	2,709	100	-24	Well Below	Well Below
Total Federal Government			+ 8					- 4		

Note: Figures may not add up to totals because of rounding.

Source: Basic data from The Budget, FY 1971, and individual agencies.

205

TABLE 53

Environment--Immediate Past and Likely Future Relative Growth

(In Millions of Dollars)

Subfunction	Total Outlays					Total R&D Conduct Expenditures				
	Dollars, 1971	Percent of Total	Percent Change, 1969-71	Growth Relative To Average 1969-71	Likely Future	Dollars, 1971	Percent of Total	Percent Change, 1969-71	Growth Relative To Average 1969-71	Likely Future
Water Pollution	465	55	+116	Well Above	Well Above	34	23	+49	Well Above	Well Above
Environmental Control	189	22	+ 43	Well Above	Well Above	82	57	+27	Well Above	Well Above
Physical Environment	199	23	+ 11	Above	Above	29	20	+13	Well Above	Well Above
Total	853	100	+ 62	Well Above	Above	145	100	+25	Well Above	Above
Total Federal Government			+ 8					- 4		

Source: Basic data from The Budget, FY 1971, and individual agencies.

to grow at rates well above the average growth rates for R&D as a whole. R&D is an important part of the Environment field, and will be used to try to find solutions to many of the problems of pollution.

CONCLUDING NOTE

A reading of the preceding material in this chapter reveals that there are relatively few instances in which the forecast of the likely future differs from the immediate past and present. Some readers will appropriately wonder whether this is an inherent result of the methodology employed. In the previous published research[2] covering 1961-69 and employing the same technique for forecasting the likely future, many more of the future estimates differed from the past. The addition of 1970 and 1971 to the present work reveals that, frequently, more changes have occurred in these years than in the previous eight years. Past experience with the technique used here is cited simply to demonstrate that the approach does not predetermine the results and that the past is frequently prologue of the future.

NOTES

1. Past general economic inflation rates are provided in Council of Economic Advisers, Annual Report (Washington, D.C.: U.S. Government Printing Office, 1970), p. 180. Implicit deflators for government purchases of goods and services are provided in U.S. Office of Business Economics, The National Income and Product Accounts of the United States, 1929-1965 (Washington, D.C.: U.S. Government Printing Office, August, 1966). Estimates of R&D inflation rates are discussed in Table 8-3, pp. 160-61, line 15.

   a. National Science Foundation, National Patterns of R&D Resources, 1953-70, NSF Publication Report No. 69-30 (Washington, D.C.: U.S. Government Printing Office, 1970).

   b. W. Halder Fisher and Leonard L. Lederman, Probable Levels of R&D Expenditures in 1970 (Columbus,

Ohio: Battelle Memorial Institute, Columbus Laboratories, December, 1969), pp. 6-7.

c.   Helen S. Milton, Cost of Research Index, 1920-1965
(Baltimore: Operations Research Society of America,
1966), XIV, 971-97.

2.   Leonard L. Lederman and Margaret L. Windus, An
Analysis of the Allocation of Federal Budget Resources as an
Indicator of National Goals and Priorities, National Aeronautics
and Space Administration, Report No. BMI-NLVP-TR-69-1
(Columbus, Ohio: Battelle Memorial Institute, Columbus
Laboratories, 1969). Available from U.S. Government print-
ing Office, Washington, D.C.

SELECTED BIBLIOGRAPHY

SELECTED BIBLIOGRAPHY

Committee for Economic Development, Research and Policy
    Committee. Budgeting for National Objectives. New
    York: Committee for Economic Development, 1966.

Dorfman, Robert, ed. Measuring Benefits of Government
    Investments. Washington, D.C.: The Brookings Institution,
    1965.

Gilpin, Robert, and Wright, Christopher. Scientists and
    National Policy Making. New York: Columbia University
    Press, 1964.

Gordon, Kermit, ed. Agenda for the Nation. Washington,
    D.C.: The Brookings Institution, 1968.

Hovey, Harold A. The Planning-Programming-Budgeting
    Approach to Government Decision-Making. New York:
    Frederick A. Praeger, 1968.

Laird, Melvin R. Fiscal Year 1971 Defense Program and
    Budget. Washington, D.C.: U.S. Government Printing
    Office, 1970.

Lecht, Leonard A. Goals, Priorities, and Dollars: The Next
    Decade. New York: The Free Press, 1966.

——. Manpower Needs for National Goals in the 1970's. New
    York: Frederick A. Praeger, 1969.

Lederman, L. L., and Windus, M. L. "An Analysis of the
    Allocation of Federal Budget Resources as an Indicator
    of National Goals and Priorities." (National Aeronautics
    and Space Administration Report No. BMI-NLVP-TR-69-1.)
    Columbus, Ohio: Battelle Memorial Institute, 1969.
    Available from the U.S. Government Printing Office,
    Washington, D.C.

National Science Foundation. "Federal Funds for Research, Development, and Other Scientific Activities, Fiscal Years 1968, 1969, and 1970." (National Science Foundation Report No. 69-31.) Washington, D. C.: U. S. Government Printing Office, 1969.

——. "National Patterns of R&D Resources: Funds and Manpower in the United States, 1958-1970." (National Science Foundation Report No. 69-30.) Washington, D. C.: U. S. Government Printing Office, 1969.

——. "Science and Engineering Doctorate Supply and Utilization, 1968-80." (National Science Foundation Report No. 69-37.) Washington, D. C.: U. S. Government Printing Office, 1969.

Novick, David, ed. Program Budgeting: Program Analysis and the Federal Budget. Cambridge, Mass.: Harvard University Press, 1965.

Organization for Economic Cooperation and Development. Reviews of National Science Policy: United States. Paris: OECD Publications, 1968.

Ott, David J., and Ott, Attiat F. Federal Budget Policy. Washington, D. C.: The Brookings Institution, 1965.

President's Commission on Budget Concepts. Report of the President's Commission on Budget Concepts. Washington, D. C.: U. S. Government Printing Office, 1967.

President's Commission on National Goals. Goals for Americans. New York: Prentice-Hall, Inc., 1960.

President's Task Force on Science Policy. Science and Technology: Tools for Progress. Washington, D. C.: U. S. Government Printing Office, 1970.

Proceedings of Trends in Science Policy. Seattle, Wash.: Battelle Seattle Research Center, 1969.

Schultze, Charles L., with Hamilton, Edward K., and Schick, Allen. Setting National Priorities, The 1971 Budget. Washington, D. C.: The Brookings Institution, 1970.

Terleckyj, Nestor E., assisted by Halper, Harriet J. Re-
    search and Development: Its Growth and Composition.
    New York: National Industrial Conference Board, 1963.

U.S. Government. The Budget of the United States Government,
    Fiscal Year 1971. Washington, D.C.: U.S. Government
    Printing Office, 1970.

——. Special Analyses, Budget of the United States, Fiscal
    Year 1971. Washington, D.C.: U.S. Government Printing
    Office, 1970.

Weidenbaum, Murray, and Saloma, John S., III. Congress
    and the Federal Budget. Washington, D.C.: American
    Enterprise Institute for Public Policy Research, 1965.

ABOUT THE AUTHORS

LEONARD L. LEDERMAN has had extensive experience
in science and technology policy, planning, and budgeting. He
is currently Deputy Head of the Office of Economic and Manpower Studies of the National Science Foundation, Washington,
D. C. This book, and the research work related to it, was
completed while he was a Fellow and Senior Research Advisor
in charge of Federal Budget and Economic Studies on the staff
of the Director of the Columbus Laboratories of the Battelle
Memorial Institute.

Mr. Lederman has served as a Consultant and Coordinator
to the President's Task Force on Highway Safety and as Executive Secretary to the National Academy of Engineering's Task
Force on Roles of the Federal Government in Applied Research.
He was Secretary to the Committee on Science and Technology
and Committee on Commercial Uses of Atomic Energy of the
Chamber of Commerce of the United States.

Mr. Lederman studied economics and engineering at the
College of the City of New York and was a fellow in the Department of Economics. He received his M. A. in economics
from New York University.

MARGARET WINDUS is on the staff of the Federal Budget
and Economics Studies group of the Battelle Memorial Institute
in Washington, D. C. Her work lies primarily in the areas of
science and technology programming and policy and R&D funding and trends. In 1969, she served as a consultant to the
President's Task Force on Highway Safety. Miss Windus was
formerly employed in the Political Science Department at the
Massachusetts Institute of Technology, assisting in studies
of the United Nations.

Miss Windus received a B. A. in Political Science from
Wellesley College and is presently studying economics at
George Washington University.